The
Guitarist and
Composer

Greg Brown
2021

All intellectual property belongs to Greg Brown

A very comprehensive book teaching the writing process and learning the guitar at the same time.

This book was inspired by my friend Mike, who has been a guitarist for many years. Mike has loved guitars and owns several. We have known each other for many years and played guitar together often. Mike writes lyrics and on many occasions asks me what would be the chords he should put to his lyrics.

As a teacher I have students that write lyrics as well and ask the same questions about chords and some ask about song structure. Many frustrated guitarist and song writers are looking for a path to understand more about the guitar, and music theory, and song form. So, I sat down and thought about how to approach learning the guitar with my friend Mike, and many of my students needs in mind. "The Guitarist and Composer" is just that!

A new way to think about learning the guitar, with the goal of writing songs, teaching the fundamentals of both in one book. This is a book that will give you direction in being a better guitarist, and helping you to know what chords, and progressions to use in your song writing.

The book starts with the very basics of music theory and understanding the guitar. Its not a beginner book, but those who have learned some of the beginning guitar fundamentals such as open chords can start in this book. Even though it starts at that level it progresses to somewhat of an advanced level towards the end. This is because many frustrated song writers need to know the answers in this book for understanding advance guitar playing and advance music theory too.

This book cannot create a hit song for anyone but it can guide you in helping you become inspired. Hit songs are birthed through inspiration and if you are inspired and become frustrated with where to go or what to do, you will find some of the answers here.

There is no particular style that this book is for, it can be used in all styles, so if you want to write pop, rock, country, metal, blues, and even jazz songs, the direction to most of it is here. Not only will you learn what you need from a theoretical stand point that information, but you will know your guitar better too, for those styles.

The "Guitarist and Composer" is your all in one source of information to learn the guitar, and how to write songs, book. I wrote it for that very purpose. It is dedicated to my friend Mike, and the students I have taught through the years wanting to know what it is in this book. Enjoy the journey.

Whats Inside

A song is born in the following ways

- A Melody

- A chord progression

- A melody and chord progression

- Mentally developing a song

How a song comes into fruition is ultimately through inspiration. The first three ways mentioned are through inspiration. The last one is using a mental concept of a song and through that, inspiration begins to take place. Having a chord progression and melody hit all at once is obviously the easiest way to compose a song. Either way a song comes to be, the elements of what it is compiled of are the same. It has a melody, a harmonic back drop, (chords) that support the melody, and it has form. Those three things can all come at once, sometimes, with the emphasis on sometimes. But, more than likely that's not going to happen often. In fact, all great song writers who have built careers on song writing, know the later to be true.

Great song writers know, it's a hard work to write songs. So, they approach it with the attitude its not through inspiration that will determine their futures as song writers. So, they have learned the art of song writing. They have mastered the elements of melody, harmony, and form. By doing this they don't rely on inspiration to come and put together the whole song all at once. They have learned how to take an idea and develop it and live with it till it becomes the songs you hear performed.

What you will learn is this study is how to take your melodies and develop them into songs, with harmony and form. This is where a lot of potential song writers are stuck. They have a melody, and some know a few chords, but have no real direction as to what chords to put with their melodies. As well as not having the ability to put chords to their melodies, they are missing direction as to how to structure their songs with form.

Identifying the challenges, you face as a song writer is what you must conquer. That requires honest introspection. So, you must ask yourself questions like the following. If I have a melody, do I know what key it is in? Do I know and understand whats involved in a key? Do I know what chords harmonically (consist of)? Do I know what major and minor chords are? Why are some chords major and minor? Why would I use a major chord or minor chord? If you cannot answer those questions, then you must be willing to study and learn those answers if you want to progress as a song writer. The only way around it is to be gifted with the ability to hear when to use major and minor chords naturally. If that were the case, you would have already put chords to your melodies.

The process of song writing must be approached with the attitude to tackle what has held you back, from putting chords to your melodies and then putting them into song form. If you're willing to work at it, you can learn the answers to what has held you back.

As the one writing this study, you are reading I have no way of knowing your challenges in the areas I mentioned. So, I have no option but to start from the very beginning for everyone reading this.

The beginning process for anyone who has a melody, myself included is to determine what key I am in. If you don't know what a key is then is difficult to take the correct approach to put chords to your melodies or improvise solos and what not.

As was mentioned some, just have a natural gift, to hear what is right. But were assuming that's not the case here and you need help. So, the beginning for you will be what is a major key, and why you need to know that.

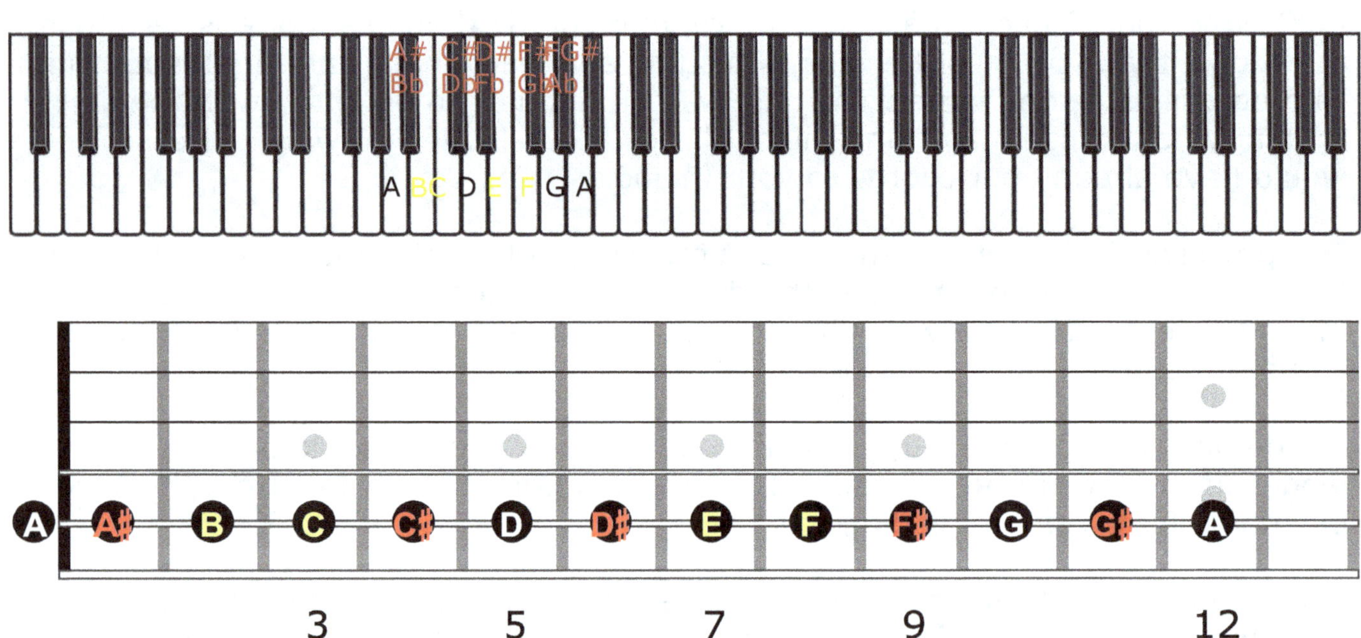

Using the Chromatic Scale

The three graphics, table, Piano keyboard, and Guitar fretboard are all illustrating the same thing. There are seven natural notes (no sharps or flats), the names are derived from the first seven letters of the Alphabet. From the letters (A B C D E F G) names are given to all notes.

From one natural note to the next is a sharp or flat note. From A to B, the note A# (Bb), comes first before you get to B. Take notice, a sharp note can be called by the letter of a flat note, one letter up.

The natural notes B and C have no other notes between them, and so does the notes E and F. All the other natural notes have sharps and flats in between them. The notes E and F and B and C are highlighted in yellow, to emphasis they are the exceptions!

When you see a series of notes as all three examples are illustrating it is called chromatic or half step movement. All three examples are the A chromatic scale. They start on A and end on A an octave higher.

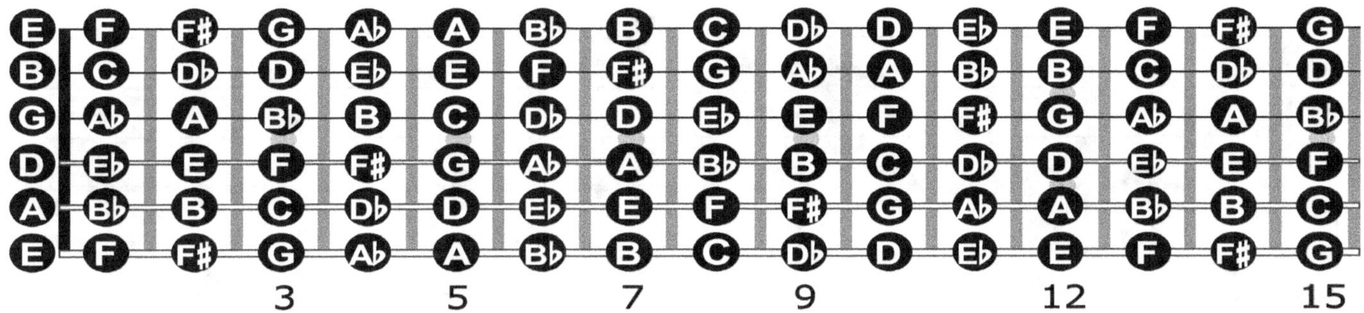

Five Chromatic Scales

The open strings on the guitar start with E, from E they proceed in a numerical pattern of four letters. From E to the fifth string A is four letters (E F G A). The sequence continues from the fifth string A to the fourth string D (A B C D). From the open string D to the third string G is four letter, (D E F G). This sequence changes to only three from the open G string to the second-string B, (G A B). From the second-string B to the first-string E, is four more letters, (B C D E).

The Lowest string and the highest string are octaves, (same note in letter name), they both are E strings.

Learning the notes on the fretboard is essential in knowing what key you are playing in if you want to apply the correct chords to your melodies. It may seem overwhelming to try to memorize all the notes on each fret, so don't! You really don't need to try to memorize what note is on each fret to know what key your in. What I mean by that is you don't have to have in your memory C is on the fourth string tenth fret, or D# is on the third string eight fret. All you need to be able to do to find what the name of any note is understand chromatic movement, that has been explained.

From the notes (E A D G B E) you have five different chromatic scales, to the 12th fret, where all the open strings repeat. If you can apply chromatic note naming from the open strings, you will learn the note names very quickly, and where they are located on all the frets. By thinking of them from chromatic movement, the process of trying to memorize them becomes easier because you will always find any note, by way of logic and not just memory. Doing it this way also helps you apply this understanding to all instruments, not just the guitar.

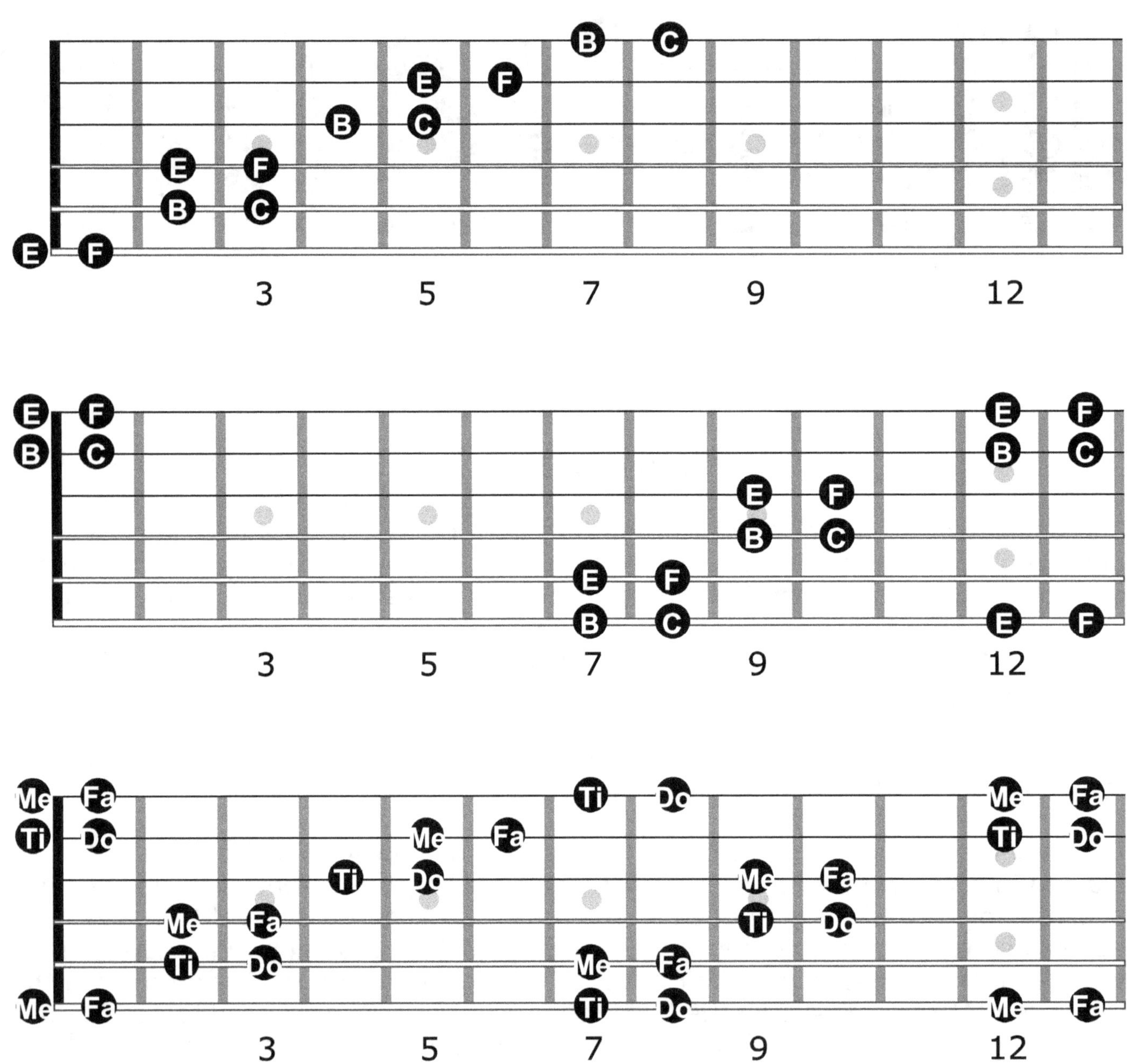

Half Steps

Starting with each open string and applying chromatic movement you will find every place on the guitar where the notes E and F and B and C are. They can be broken down to two horizontal patterns. When the two patterns are combined, they form the full image of those notes that the third diagram is showing.

These two patterns are the half steps that are in the C major scale. Whole and half steps create major scales from any chromatic scale. The notes of the C major scale are the foundation for the entire key of C. The notes in the C major scale are (C D E F G A B C).

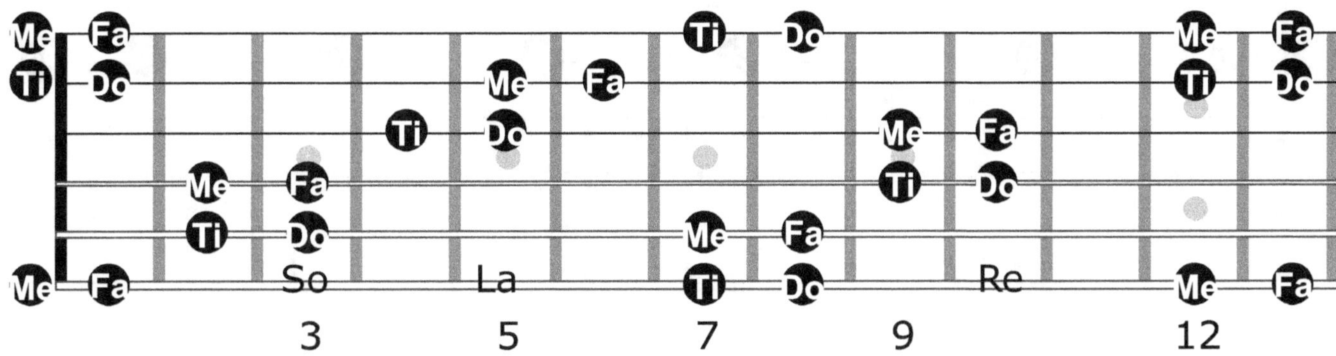

Do	Re	Me	Fa	So	La	Ti	Do
1	2	3	4	5	6	7	8
C	D	E	F	G	A	B	C

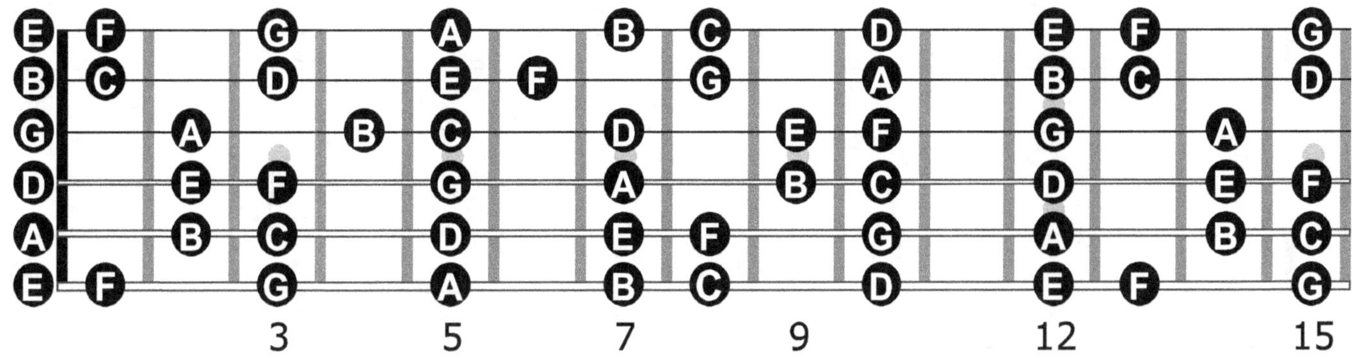

Forming the Major Scale

You could substitute the letters with (Do Re Me Fa So La Ti Do). The notes E and F are (Me and Fa), the notes (B and C are (Ti and Do). Once, you substitute the syllables for note names, you don't have to memorize every note in a major key to play them on any string.

From the half steps Me and Fa, there are two whole steps, they are the notes So, and La. From the half steps, Ti and Do, there is only Re. Once you can find the half steps on a string you can complete the missing whole steps, and determine the key you are in. Where Do is will be the name of the key.

Knowing the key you are in with your melody, you can start the process of applying chords to your melody. But in order to complete this process you have to know the rules for chords in major keys. Then you can have the direction you need to harmonize your melodies with chords from the major key you are in.

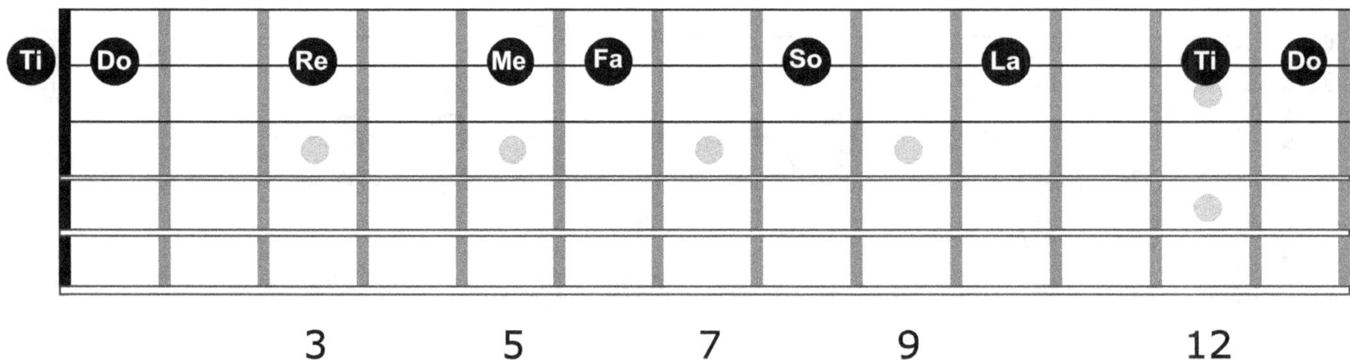

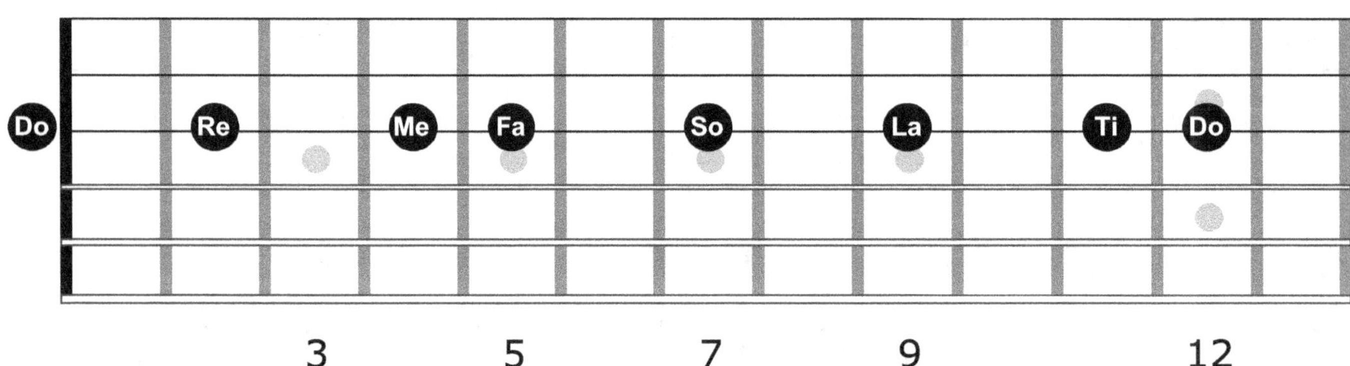

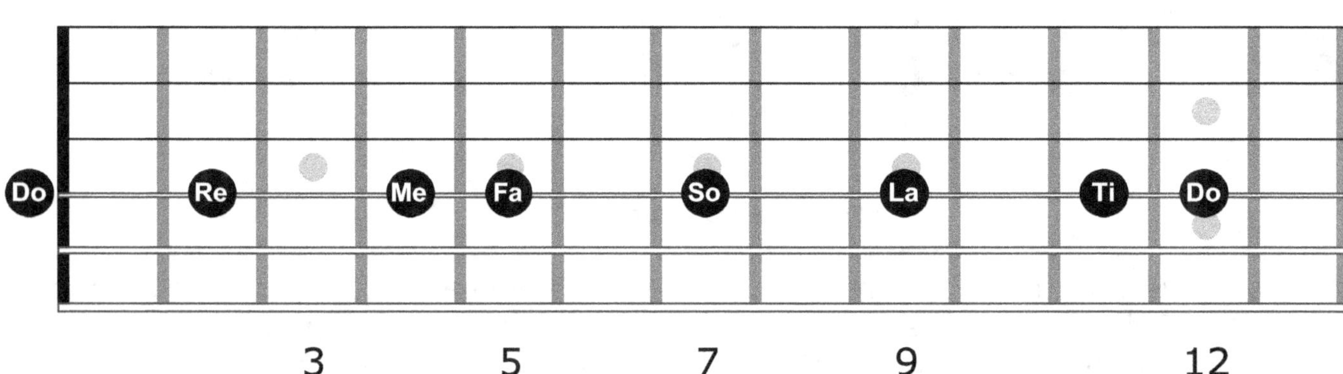

Do	Re	Me	Fa	So	La	Ti	Do
1	2	3	4	5	6	7	8
C	D	E	F	G	A	B	C
G	A	B	C	D	E	F#	G
D	E	F#	G	A	B	C#	D

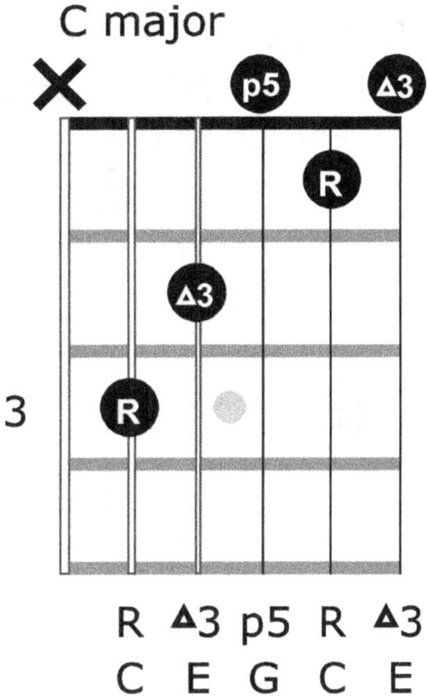

Understanding the Major Chord

A major chord in its basic structure has three different notes. These three notes are called triads. The notes (C E G) form the C major triad. It is called C, for the reason the note C, is the fundamental note. The Fundamental note is also called the root note, as shown with the letter R.

The triad can have repeats of any or all of the three notes. The triad can also be in various orders from one note to the next too. The note C (root note) does not have to be the lowest note, but in many cases it is. If the root note is not the lowest note it is called an inversion. When the third is the lowest note, the chord is called first inversion. When the fifth is the lowest note it is called second inversion.

The major chord will produce a happy bright sound in comparison to other types of chords. This is important to know because it gives an indication of the feeling, emotionally you are applying it to in a song.

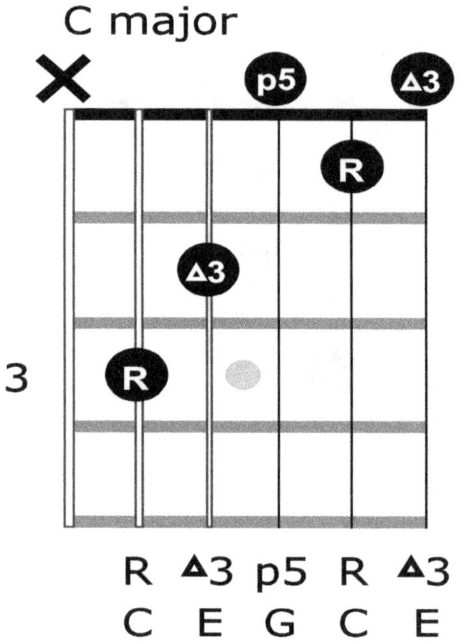

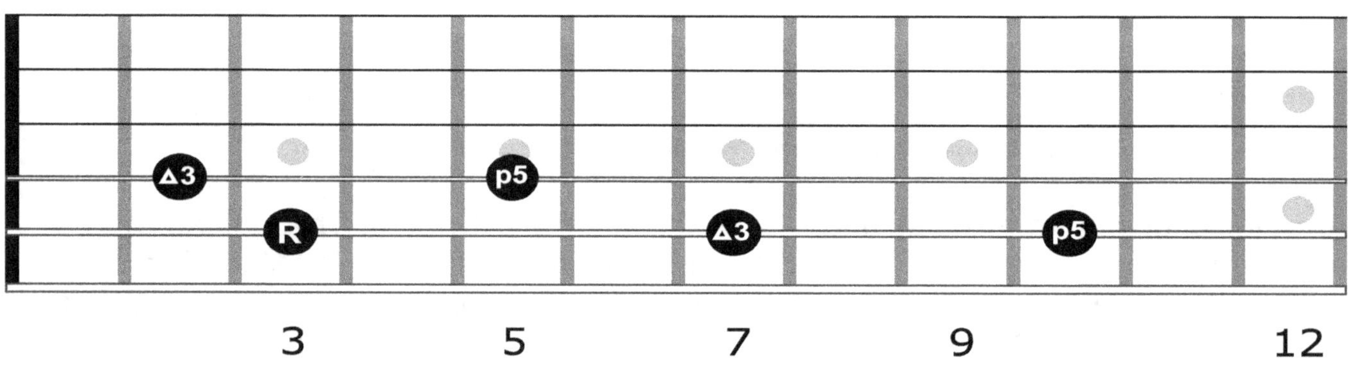

Major Third Interval

 The major chord is formed and named because it has the major third interval from the root note. From one fret to the next either up or down, is what is called a half step, or minor second interval. Two frets in ether direction from one note to the next is a major second interval.

From the note C to the note C sharp is one fret, and that is a minor second interval. From the note C to the note D is a major second, and that is two frets up from C. From the note C to the note E, on the seventh fret, is a major third. A minor third would be from C to the note E flat on the sixth fret. The major third interval is two whole steps from the root of a major chord.

The major third can be played on adjacent strings five and four, because of the way the guitar is tuned. This way you can play the major third and other intervals from one adjacent string to the next.

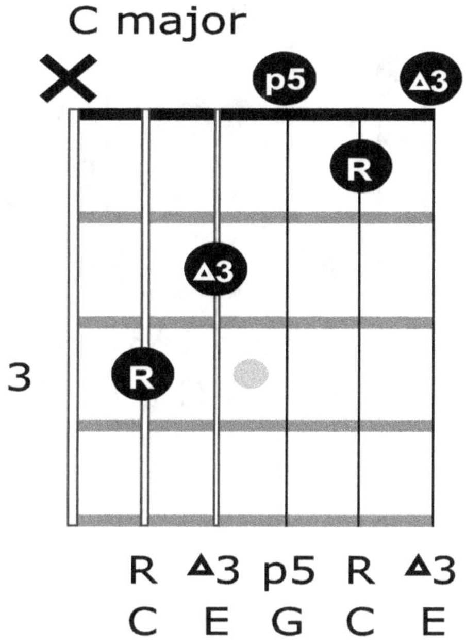

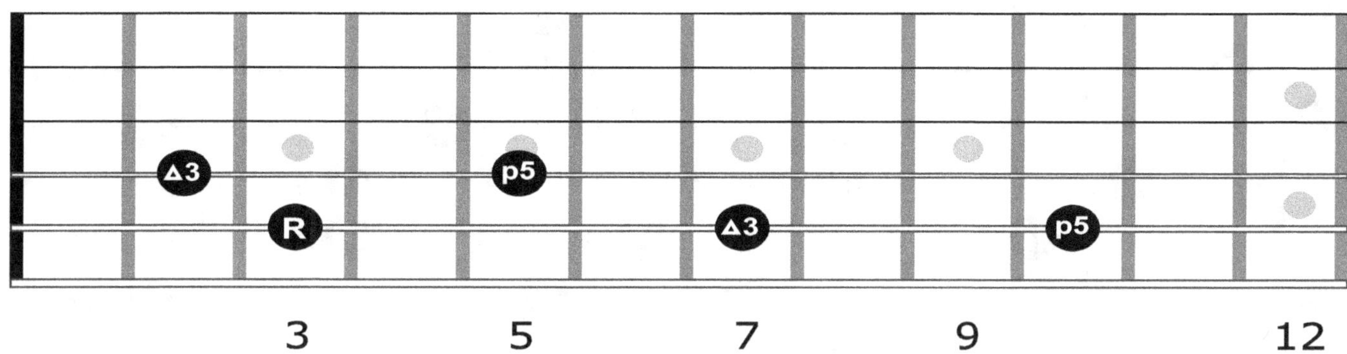

Perfect Fifth Interval

The perfect fifth interval can be thought of as the distance of the major third and from the major third, a minor third, combined from the root. From C to G, is a perfect fifth. The fretboard diagram directly above is illustrating the E and G notes on the fifth string, are the same notes in sound or pitch, as the E and G notes are on the fourth string.

The open G on the third string, first diagram (C major Chord) is the same in sound as the other two G notes on the second diagram. The C on the second string and open E note are octaves of C and E.

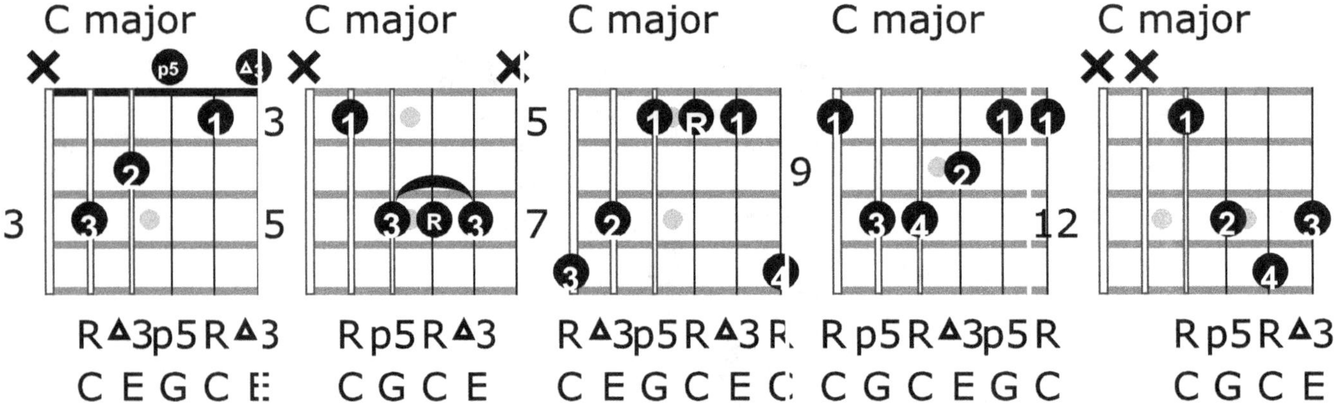

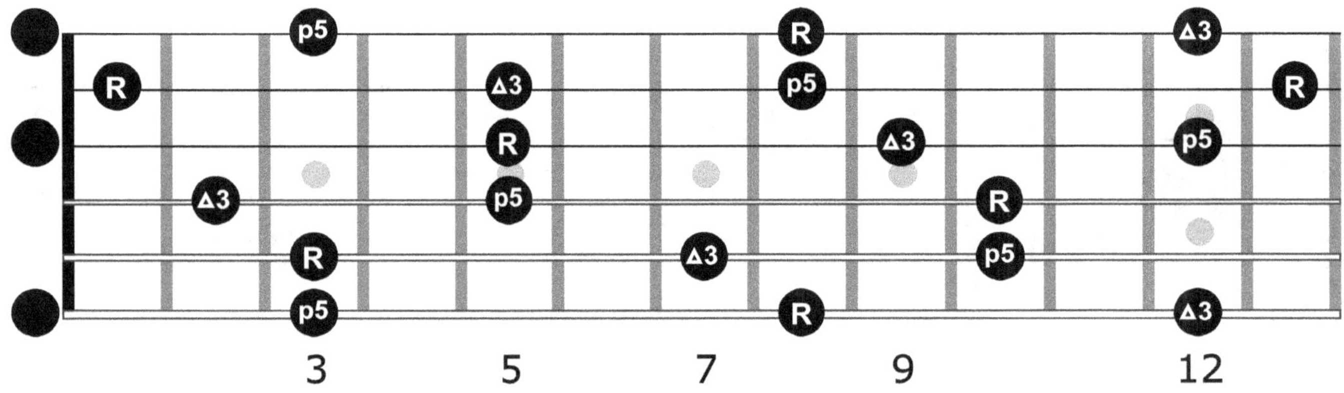

Five Chord Shapes

As a song writer, you can play a chord using any chord shape you want, so its not necessary to know all of them, to put chords to your lyrics, or melodies. These chord shapes are how many guitarists see the C, chord as well as all chords on the fretboard. These five shapes for the C major chords can be moved to different locations to play all major chords. This is known as the "C A G E D system".

The various ways you play a chord will sound different from one another, because the way the order of the notes is arranged. The main thing is they are all just the notes (C E G).

The chords on this page are here for you to learn if you want but it should be understood you do not need to know them all to play a major chord.

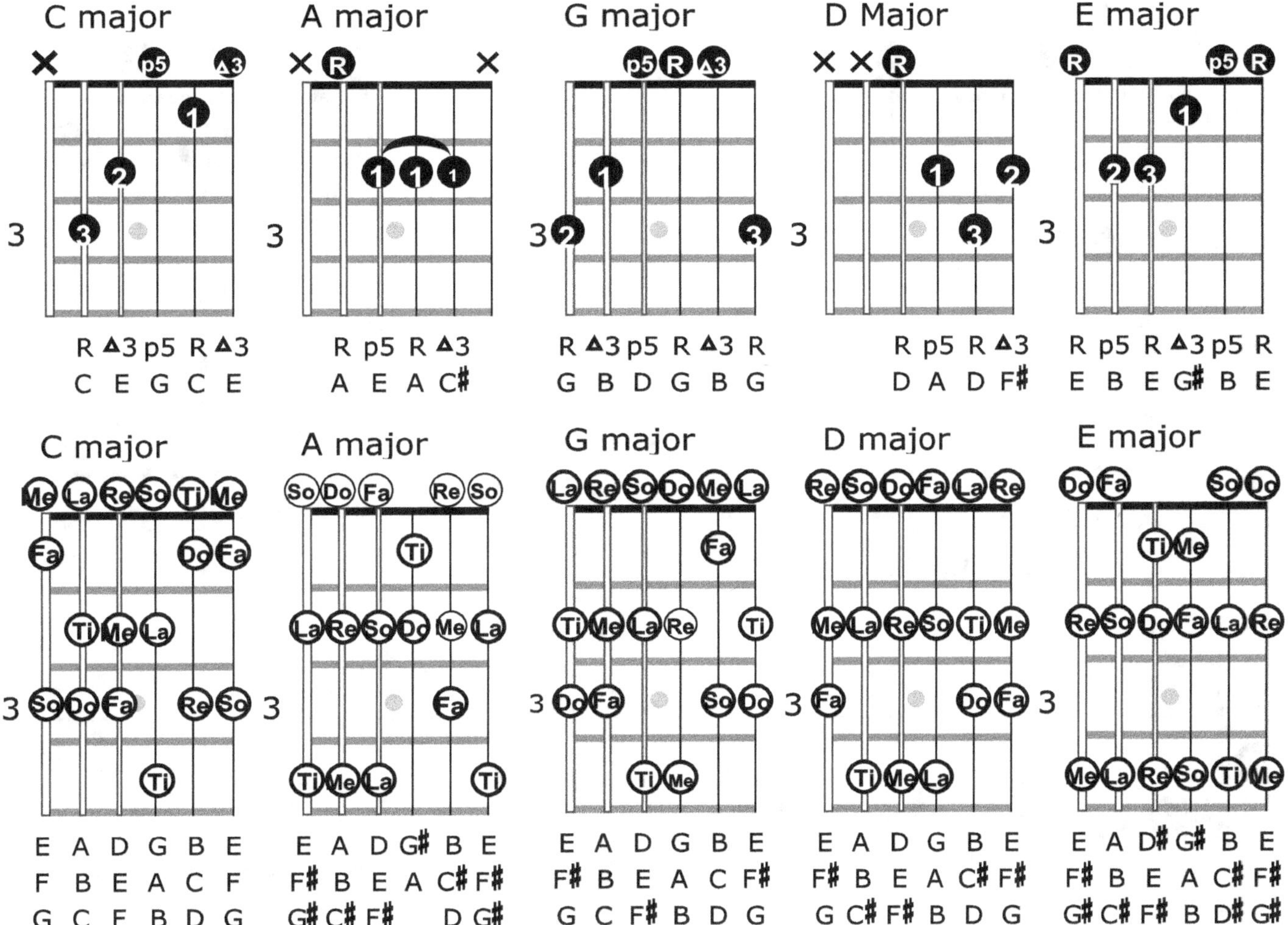

Using Open Chords and Scales

The five major chords and their root scales are what most guitarist know, in the open position. These major chords are used in a lot of songs. It would be great practice to know the other notes in the second row that are where the chords are derived from.

All major chords are constructed with the same intervals that was illustrated with the C major chord. From the root a major third and a perfect fifth. As a song writer you can play the notes around these five chords, from their root scales and create melodies and hear what the root chords from them sounds like.

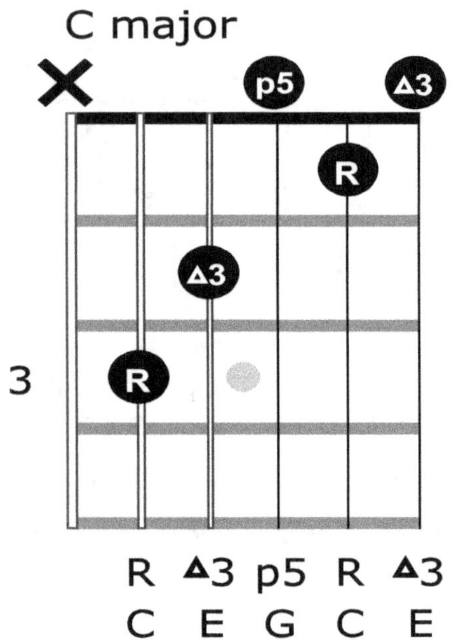

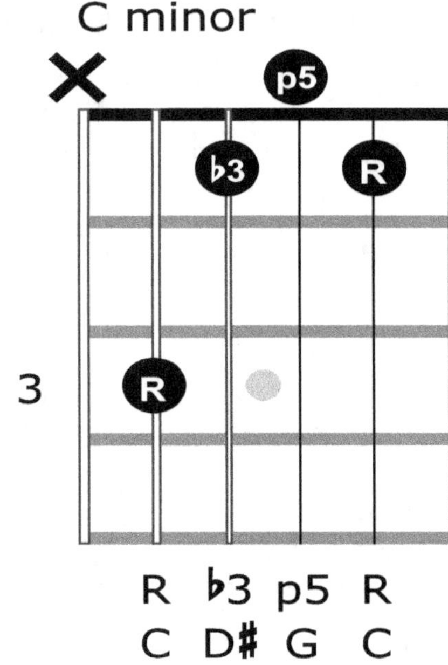

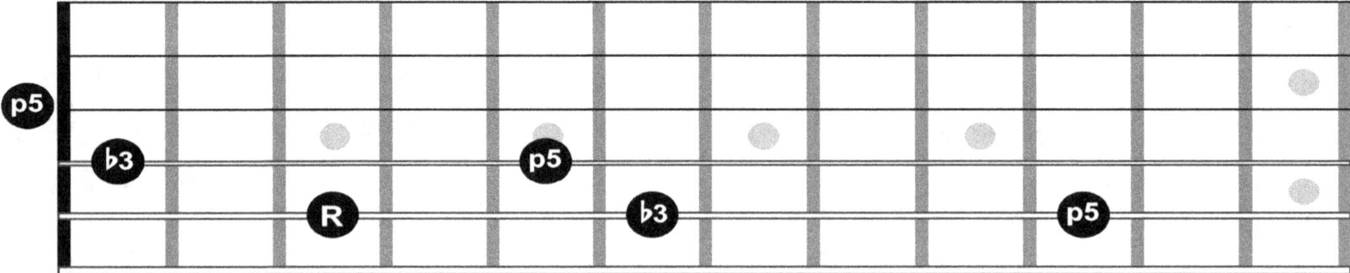

Comparing Major and Minor Chords

The minor chord has a darker feel to it then the major chord. Major and minor chords together are used for harmonizing melodies.

The minor chord has only one note different from the major chord. The third of the major chord is lowered a half step to form the minor chord. The interval of the perfect fifth from the root remains the same. The minor third to the perfect fifth, creates a major third interval from those notes.

In comparison to the major third to the perfect fifth forms a minor third interval. Comparing the C major to C the minor chord, you can see the lowered third. The third of any major chord can be lowered a half step to create a minor chord.

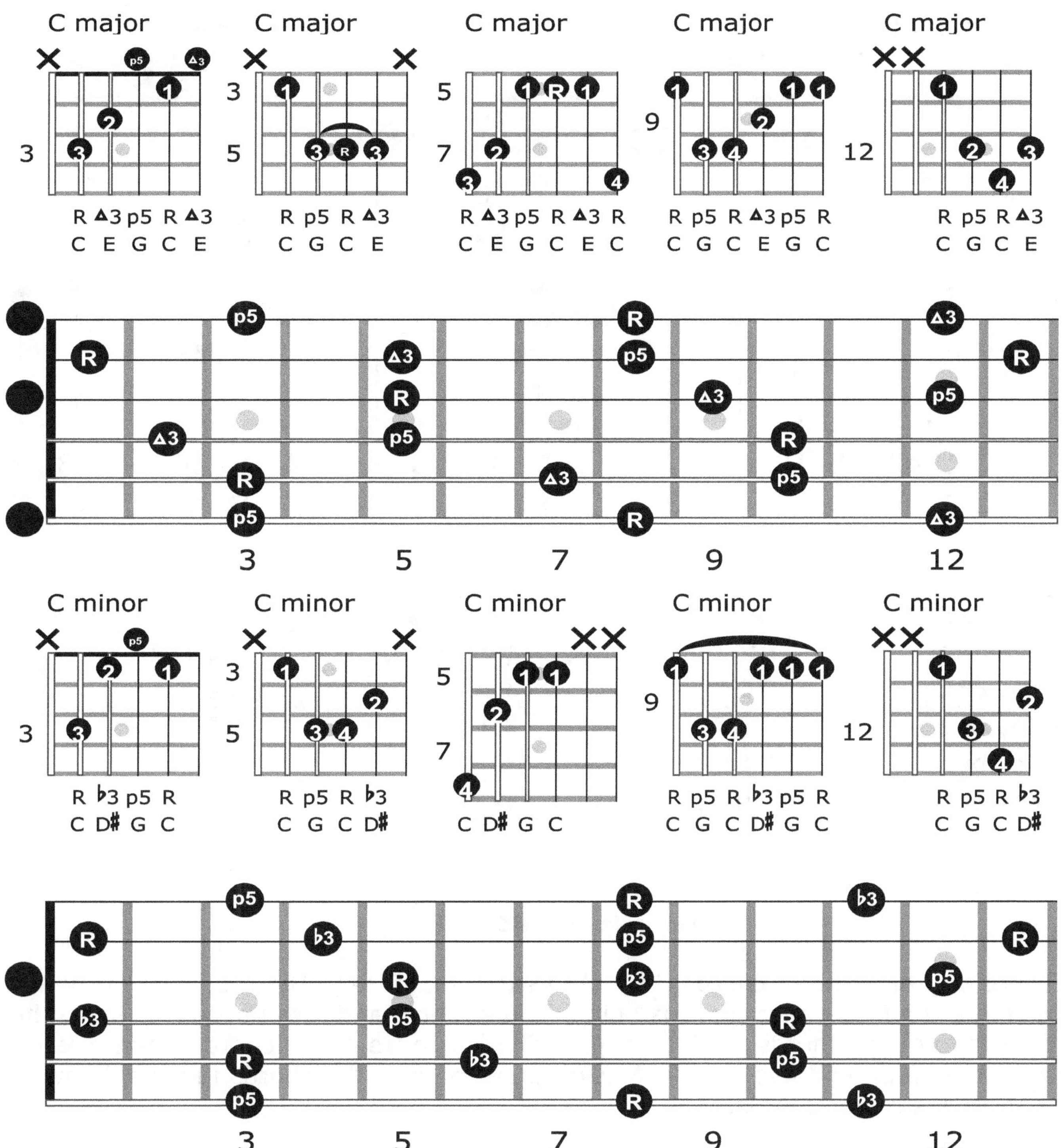

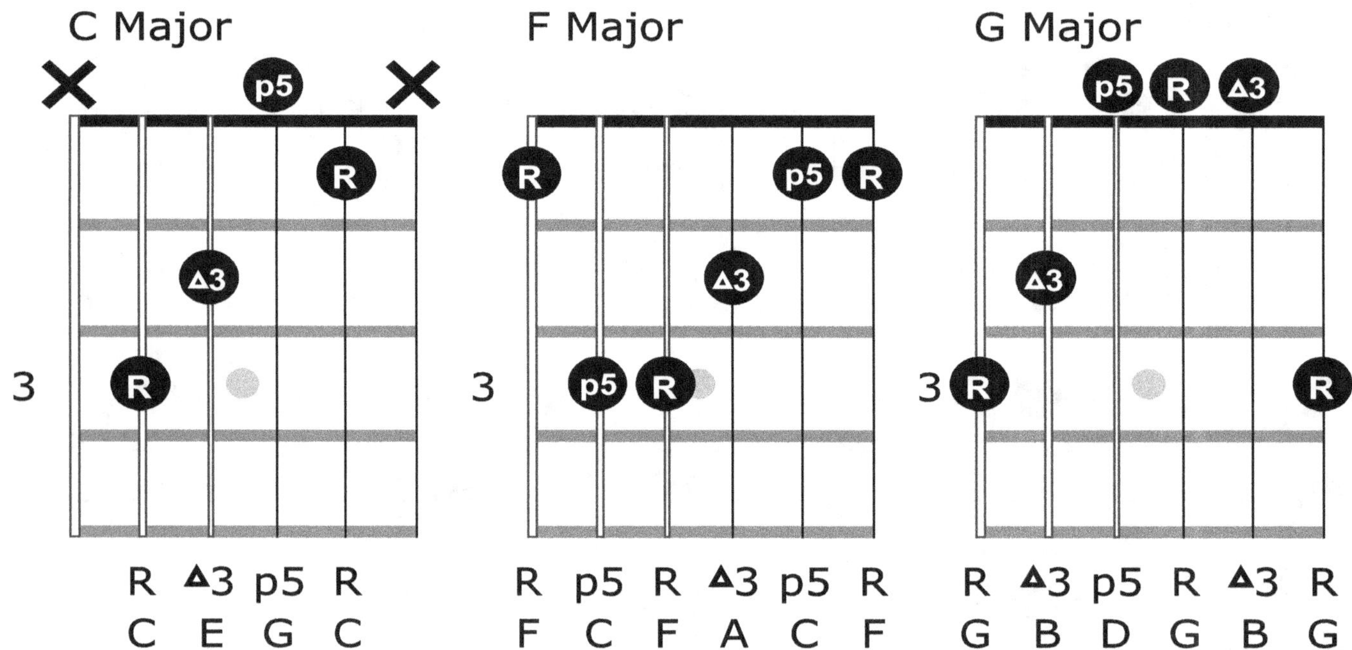

Key and Chord Function	One (Do) (Do Me So)	Four (Fa) (Fa La Do)	Five (So) (So Ti Re)
Key of C	C E G	F A C	G B D
Key of G	G B D	C E G	D F# A
Key of D	D F# A	G B D	A C# E
Key of A	A C# E	D F# A	E G# B

Primary Chords (1 4 5)

There are three major chords (triads) in every major key. The root note of the key is where the first major chord is built on. The fourth and fifth notes are where the other two major chords are found. You will hear these major chords often referred to as one, four, and five chords. Musicians, who know the chords in keys, know that means major chords.

Its important to know what notes in a major a key are in each triad. This way when you are wanting to put major chords to a melody, you can choose the right major chord, from the key.

A real helpful tip to know how to put major chords together in a song, is to remember any two major chords a whole step apart are the four and five chords of a major key.

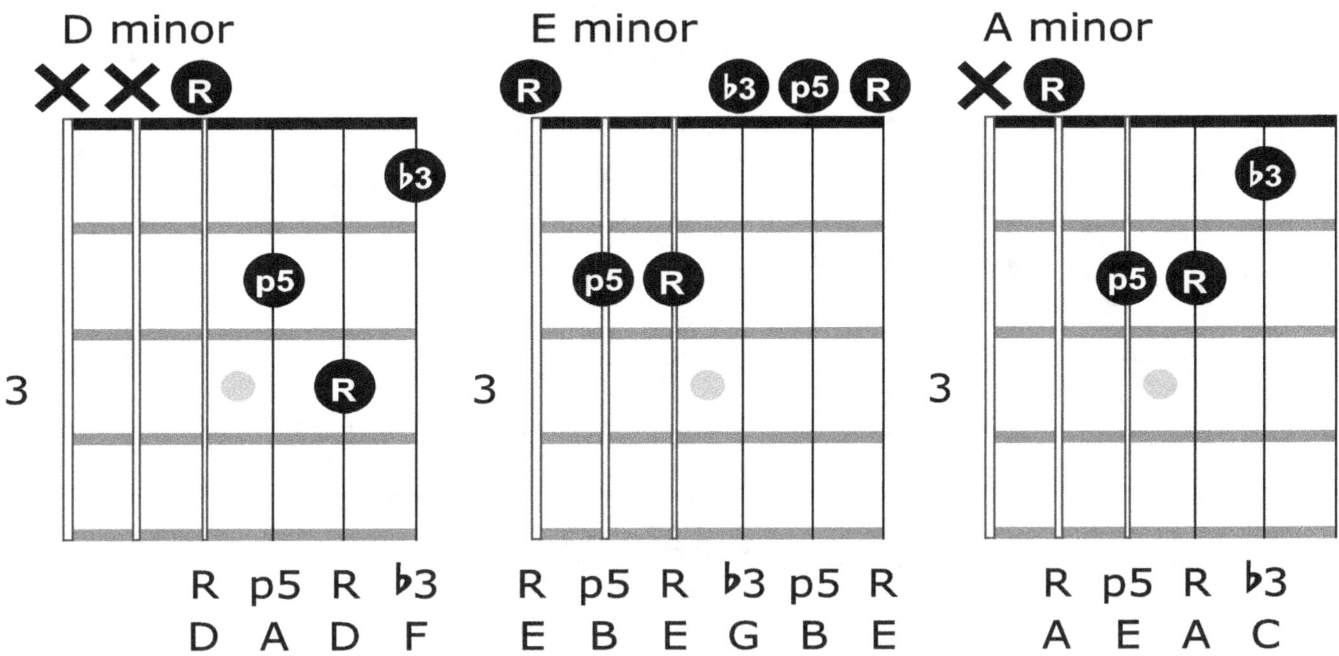

Key and Chord Function	two Re) (Re Fa La)	Three (Me) (Me So Ti)	Six (La) (La Do Me)
Key of C	D F A	E G B	A C E
Key of G	A C E	B D F#	E G B
Key of D	E G B	F# A C#	B D F#
Key of A	B D F#	C# E G#	F# A C#

Minor Chords (2 3 6)

The minor chords in every major key are found on the second, third, and sixth scale degrees of the major scale. Its just as important to know the notes from the scale that form each minor chord. This way you can use the correct minor chord in a key to support your melody you are singing or putting chords too.

A helpful tip in using minor chords, is to know two minor chords a whole step apart are the second and third chords of the major key.

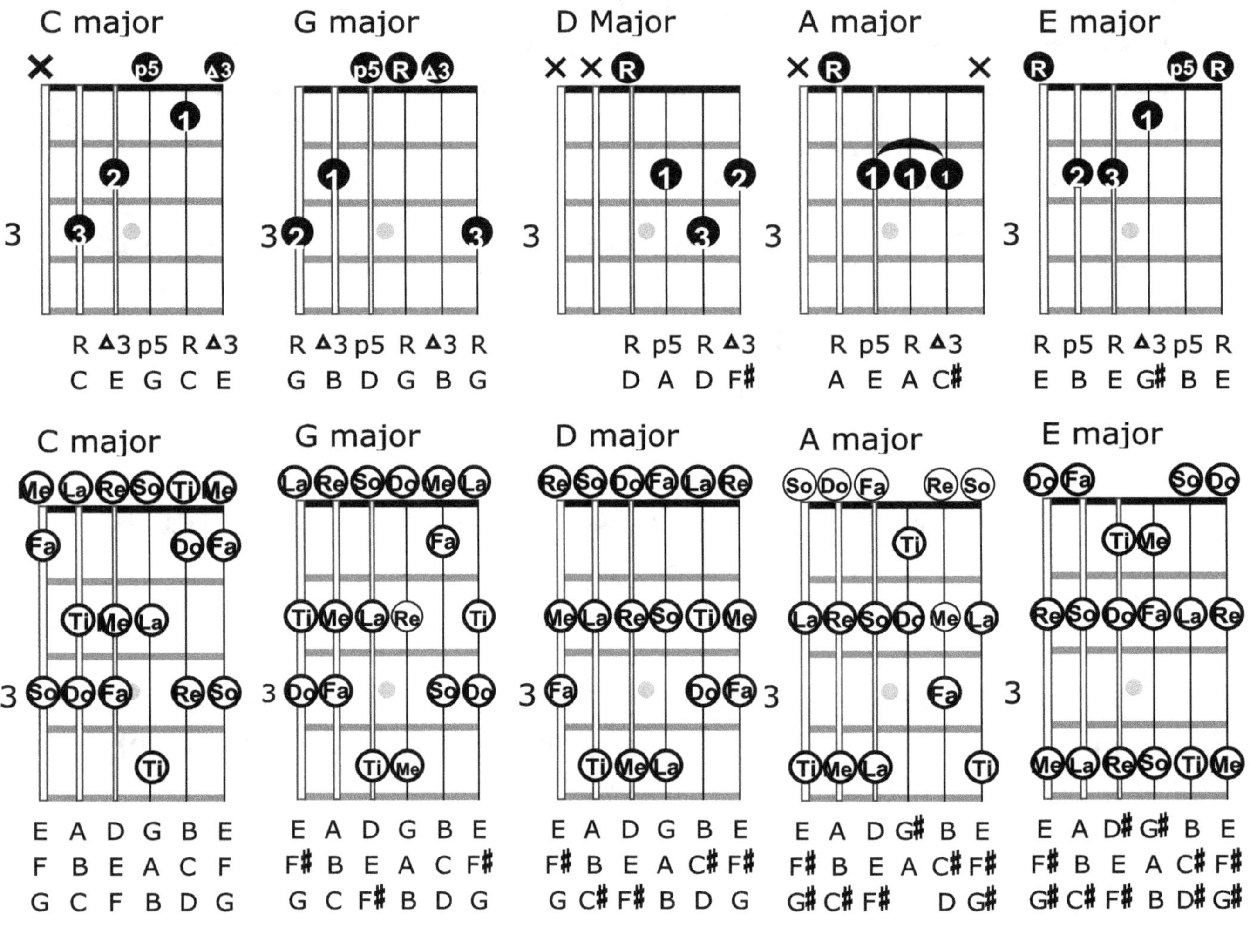

Do	Re	Me	Fa	So	La	Ti	Do
C	D	E	F	G	A	B	C
G	A	B	C	D	E	F#	G
D	E	F#	G	A	B	C#	D
A	B	B#	D	E	F#	G#	A
E	F#	G#	A	B	C#	D#	E

Singing Scales

Find a comfortable scale and starting place in one of the five keys above and sing and play Do to the octave of that Do. For example start on the Do on the fifth string third fret with the C major scale and sing that Do to the second string first fret Do, without repeating any two syllables before the octave.

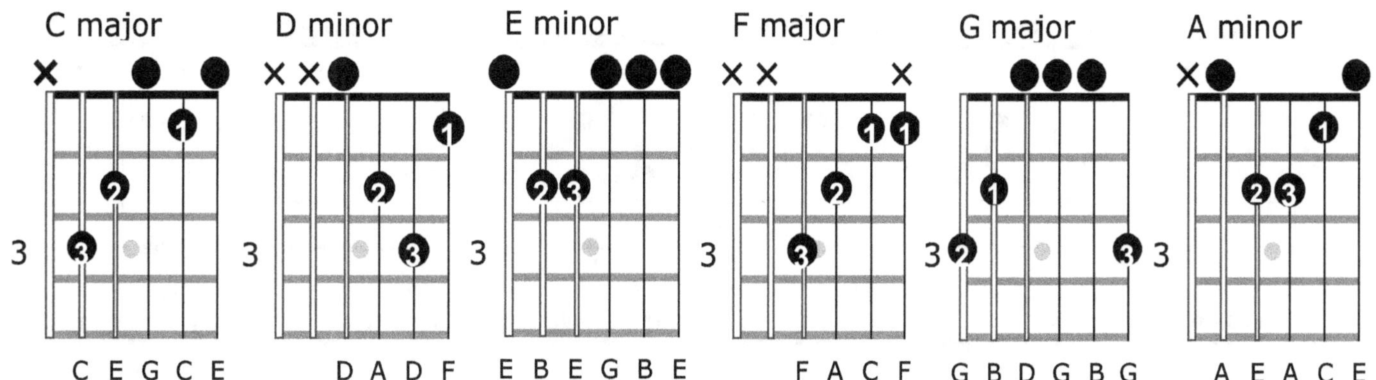

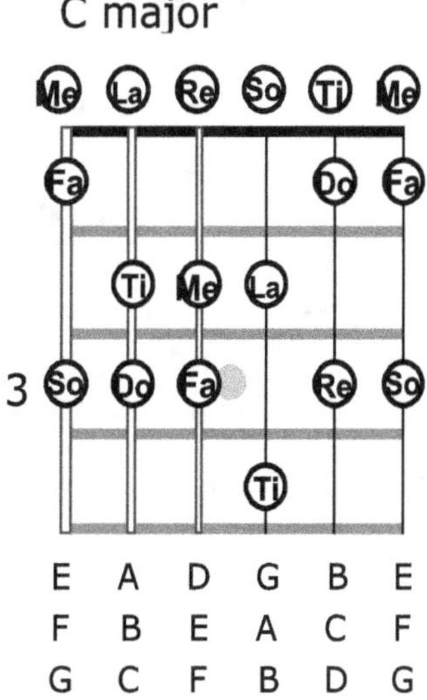

C major	Do	Re	Me	Fa	So	La	Ti	Do
D minor	Re	Me	Fa	So	La	Ti	Do	Re
E minor	Me	Fa	So	La	Ti	Do	Re	Me
F major	Fa	So	La	Ti	Do	Re	Me	Fa
G major	So	La	Ti	Do	Re	Me	Fa	So
A minor	La	Ti	Do	Re	Me	Fa	So	La

Chords and melodies

Play each chord and then play or sing the corresponding syllables. This will help you start to get some understanding of what chords to put to your melodies with your songs. Listen to how each chord sounds with the scale that is related to the chord. For example the C chord starts and ends on Do. The D minor chord starts and ends on Re, and so on.

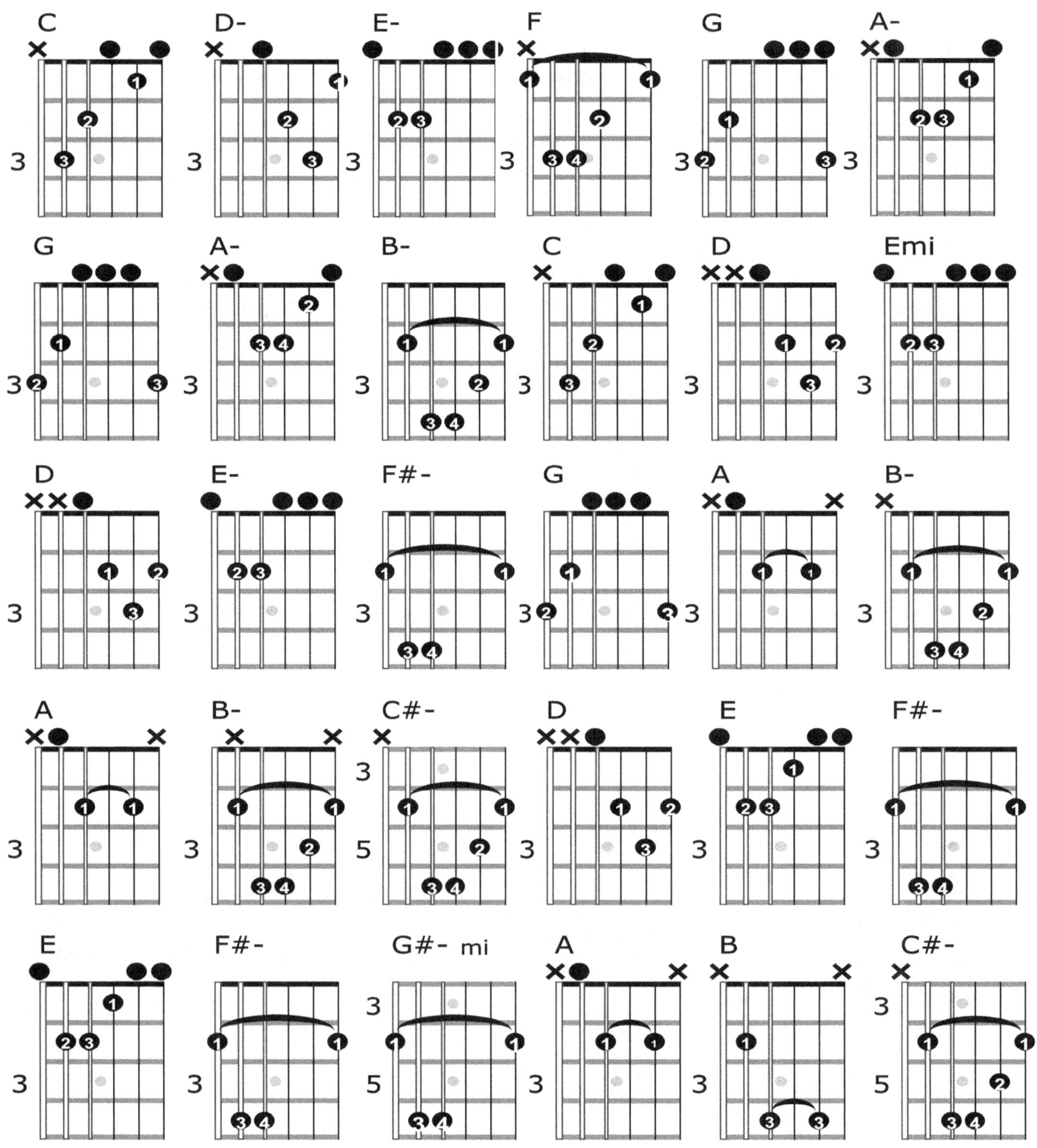

Chords (1 2 3 4 5 6) in the Major Keys

The Chords for each key are the one, two, three, four, five, and six chords. The keys are C, G, D, A, and E.

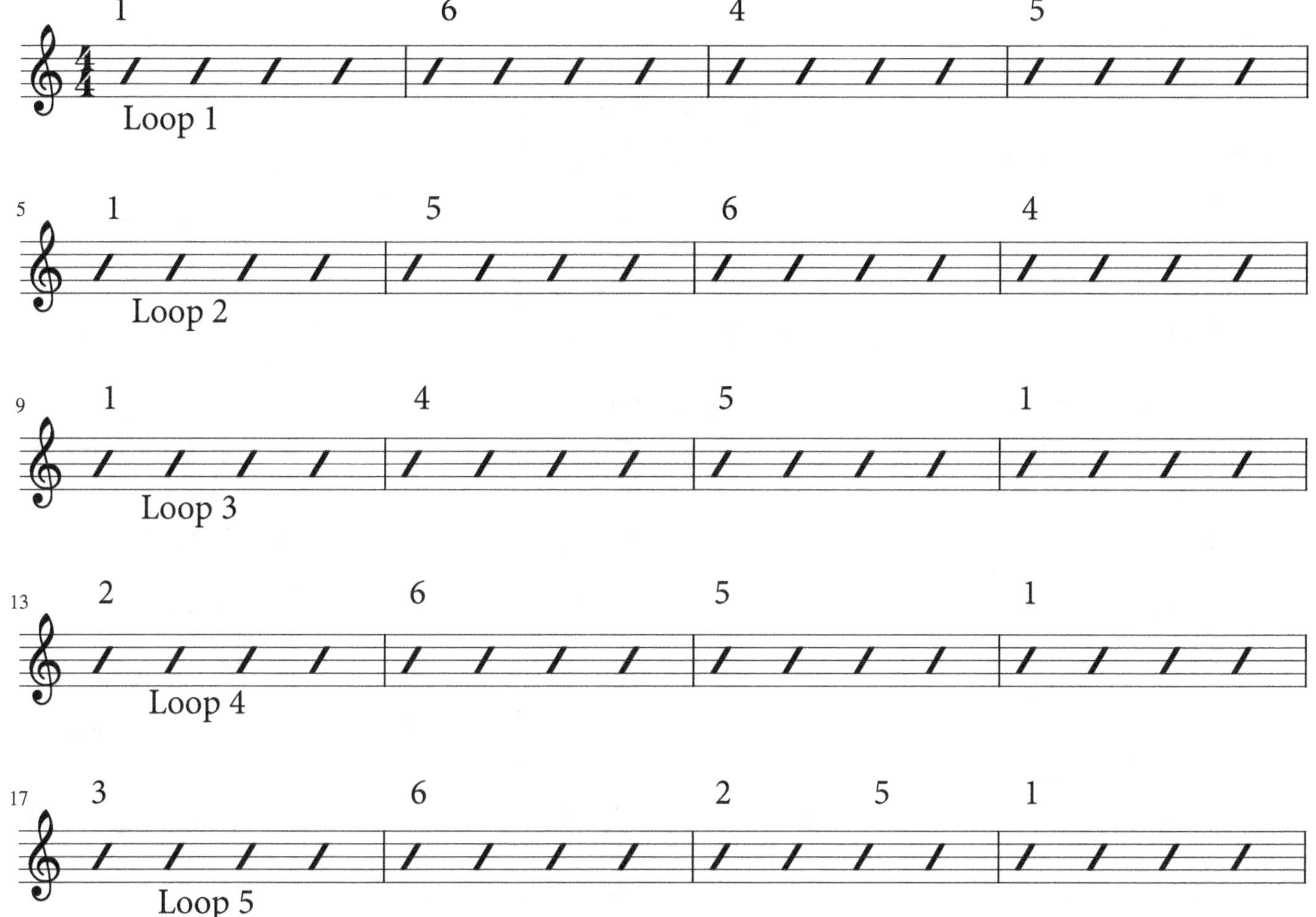

Popular Loops (Chord Progressions)

The numbers above the measures are there to represent the one through six chords in the major key. You can apply these loops to any key by just knowing the chords for that key with the numbers one through six.

Loops and measures are just a means to bring organization to song writing. A loop could represent your verses. The chorus could be another loop. A loop can be any combination of chords it all depends on what you are singing for a melody. But understanding keys, and chord functions in a key, added to creating loops, now gives better organized thought, in the song writing process.

Practice the loops with four beats to each measure and strum the chords with four counts to each measure.

G major

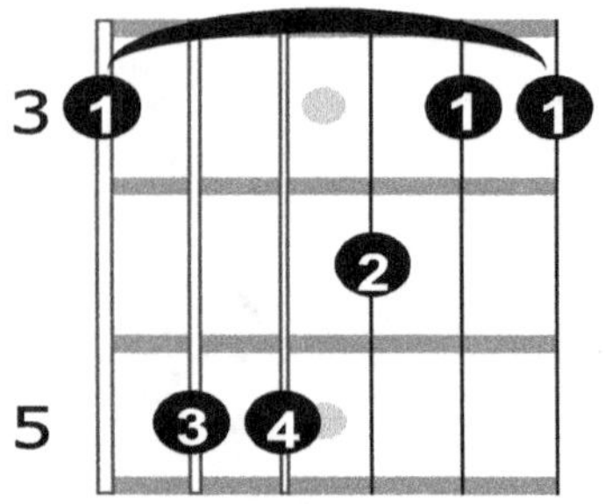

R p5 R △3 p5 R
G D G B D G

A minor

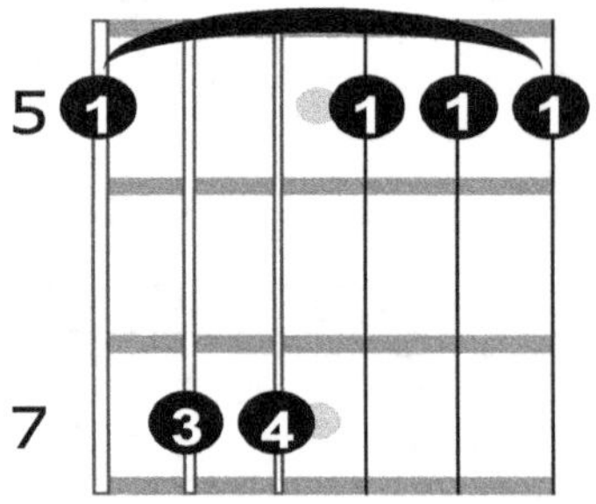

R p5 R ♭3 p5 R
A E A C E A

B minor

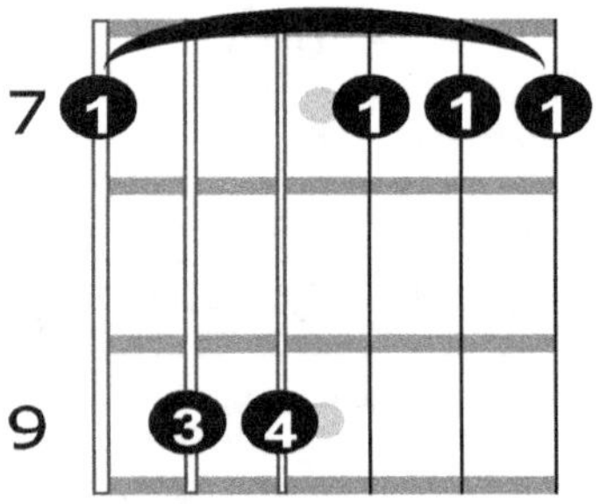

R p5 R ♭3 p5 R
B F♯ B D F♯ B

C major

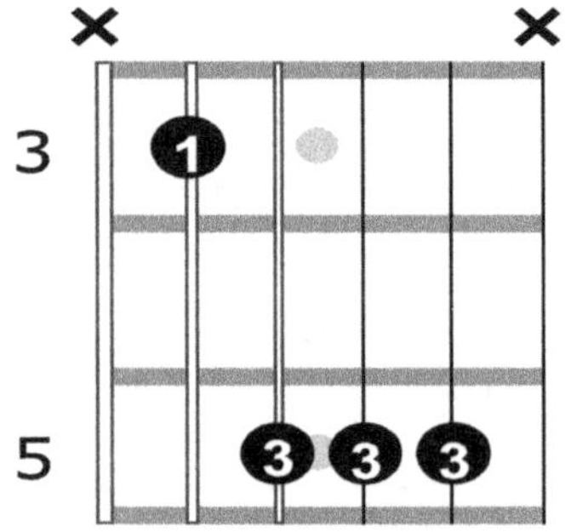

R p5 R △3
C G C E

D major

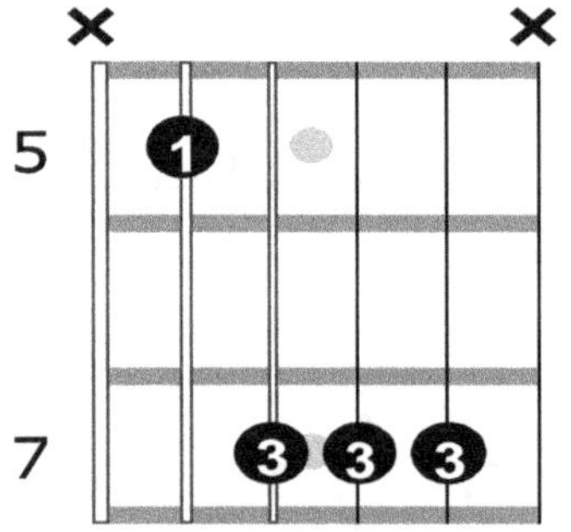

R p5 R △3
D A D F♯

E minor

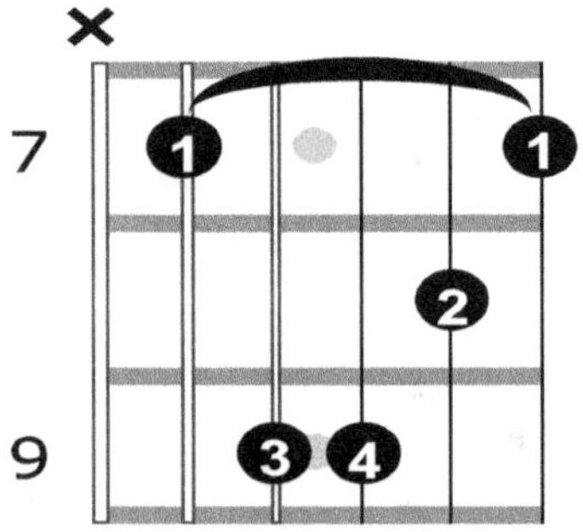

R p5 R ♭3 p5
E B E G B

Chords 1- 6

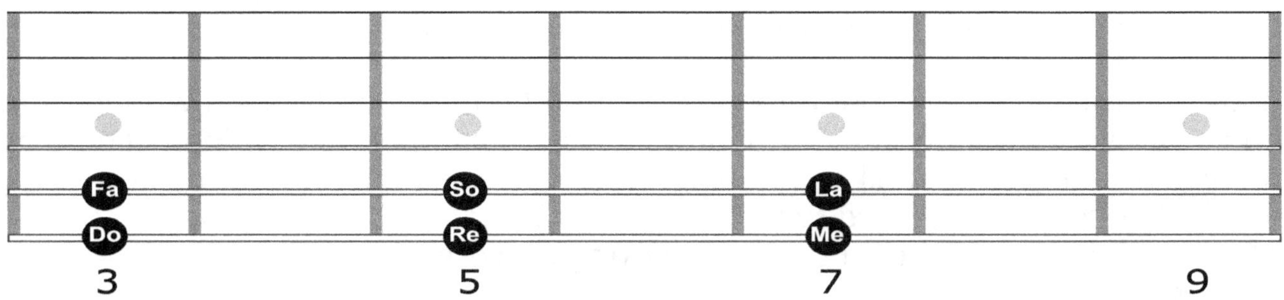

Root Patterns for 6th and 5th Strings

The pattern on the sixth string is for the one, two, and three chords. The pattern on the fifth string is for the four, five and six chords.

Using just the root and fifth of each chord you can play power chords too.

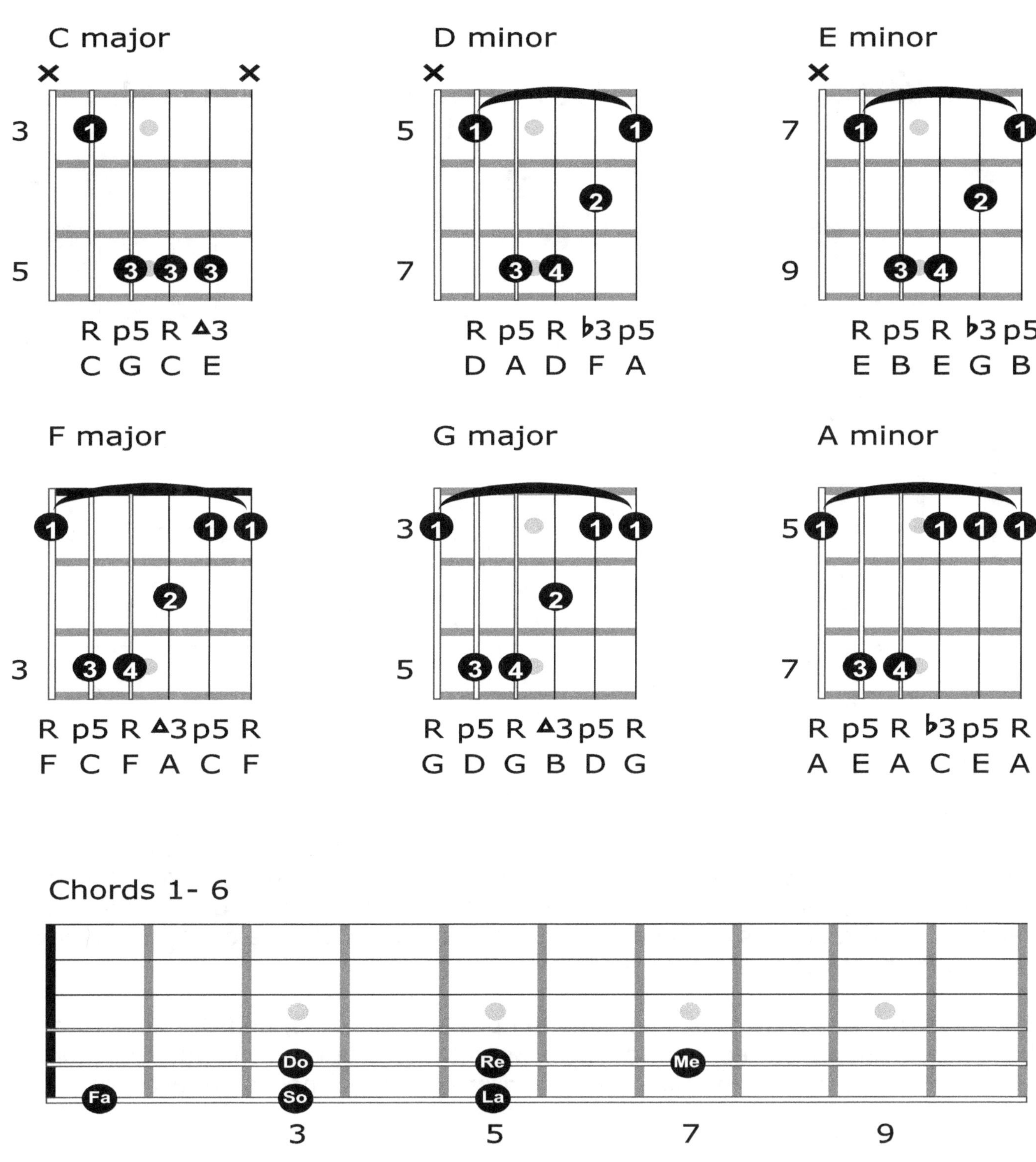

Root Patterns for 5th and 6th Strings

The pattern on the fifth string is for the one, two, and three chords. The pattern on the sixth string is for the four, five and sixth chords.

The root and fifth of these chords can be used to play power chords too.

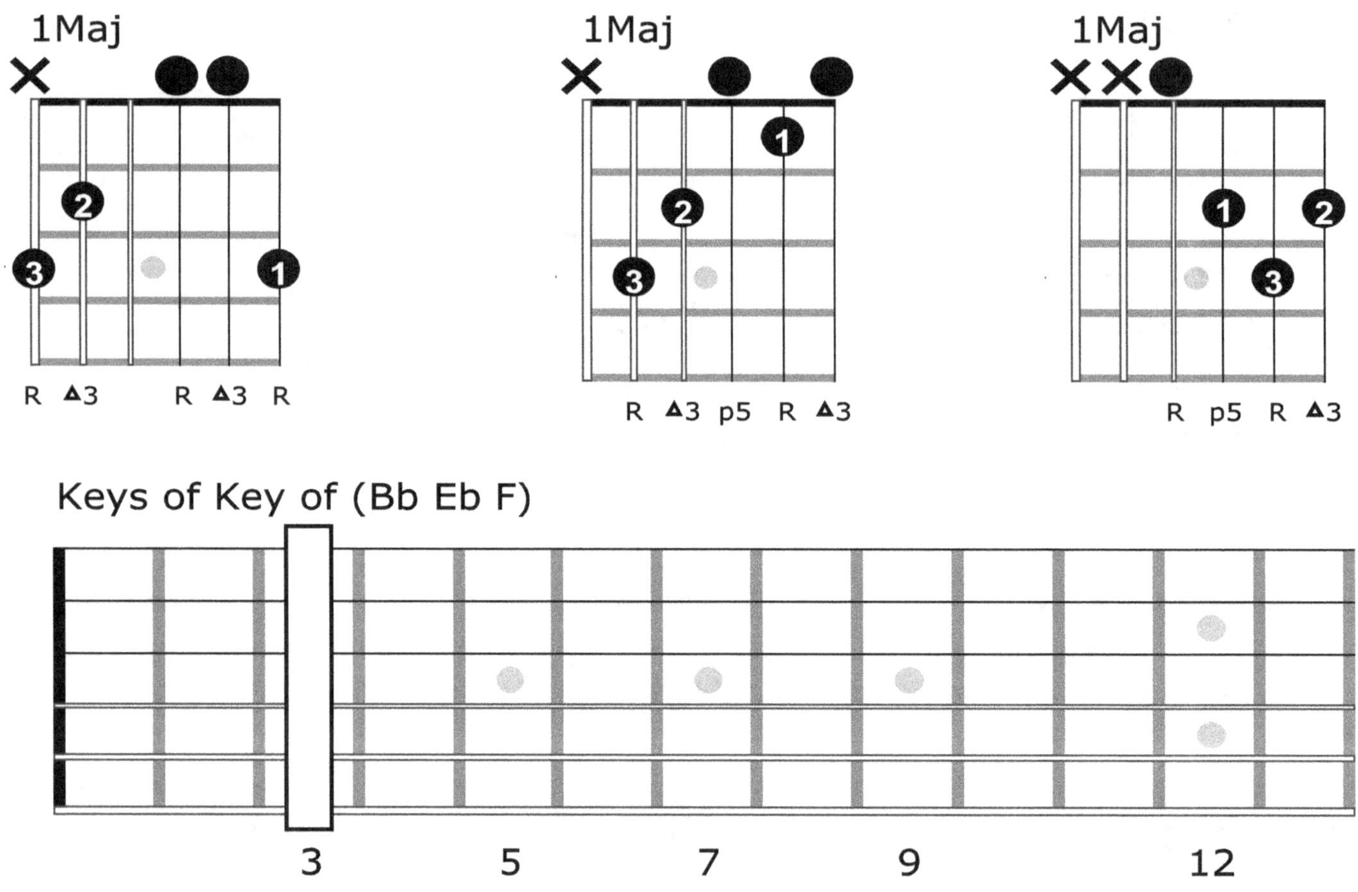

Why a Capo is Used

Many singer song writers do not use bar chords, and in fact they have a very limited knowledge of chords beyond the open position. But, because the keys they sing in are not keys, that are easily played in the open position, they use a capo. The capo moves the guitar's open position to any fret and therefore changes the key, that open chords can be played in.

The keys that are easy to play in the open position are C, G, and D. These three keys can be easily moved with the capo. With the use of the capo and the chord shapes in those keys, every key a song writer and singer needs are accessible to them.

The root notes for the chords in the open position remain on the same strings only the open position has now been moved. For example, if the capo is on the third fret, and you move all the open chords for the key of G to that new open position, you would be in the key of Bb. If you move all the open chords for C, you would be in the key of Eb. If you moved all the open chords for D, you would be in the key of F. This is one of the reasons the capo is used.

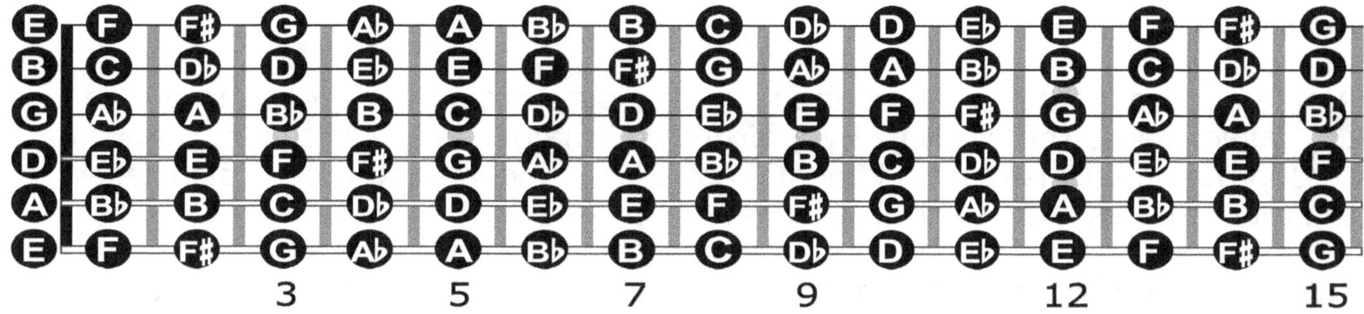

What You Should be able to Do

The understanding you have gained of the major key and its chords, is just the beginning of your foundation. The diagram above has all the notes on the fretboard up to the fifteenth fret. You can see the notes all repeat at the twelfth fret. Each note can be a root note for a major key. This would give you twelve different notes for the major keys. Enharmonic notes for example G# (Ab) are the same. This gives you seven natural root notes for keys, and five root notes for sharp keys and five root notes for flat keys. Sharp and flat keys can be the same notes en harmonically.

If you sing a melody and use the lessons in half steps, you have two choices, for the two half steps to use, to determine the key. They are the third and fourth notes (Me and Fa) or the seventh and eight notes (Ti and Do). They will lead you to the root of the key or the note (Do).

Once you find the key then you apply the rules for the key as far as chords go. The one, four, and five chords, are major, the two, three, and six chords are minor. The seventh chord is a diminished chord, and for now will not be included in application.

The chords were structured from the major key with three major chords and three minor chords, in the way they are because all the triads must remain in the key. If a major chord was on the second degree it would have a major third interval and that would be out of the normal boundaries of the major key.

The options you can choose from now as far as chords and keys are concerned should help you begin to apply basic chords to some of your melodies. The use of bar chords, and capos, will be helpful to some but the knowledge of both will prove useful.

Major Chords

A major chord in its basic structure has three different notes. These three notes are called triads. The notes (C E G) form the C major triad. It is called C, for the reason the note C, is the fundamental note. The fundamental note is also called the root note, as shown with the letter R.

The triad can have repeats of any or all of three notes. The triad can also be in various orders from one note to the next too. The note C (root note) does not have to be lowest note, but in many cases it is.

The major chord is formed and named because it has the major third interval from the root note. From one fret to the next either up or down, is what is called a half step, or minor second interval. Two frets in either direction from one note to the next is a major second interval.

Minor Chords

The minor chord has only one note different from the major chord. The third of the major chord is lowered a half step to form the minor chord. The interval of the perfect fifth from the root remains the same. The minor third to the perfect fifth, creates a major third interval from those notes. In comparison to the major third to the perfect fifth forms a minor third interval.

Major Key

A major key has seven different notes that are put together by a formula of two whole steps from the root, then one half step, then three more whole steps and one more half step. The half steps are from the notes three and four, and seven and eight.

There are three major chords (triads) in every major key. The root note of the key is where the first major chord is built on. The fourth and fifth notes are where the other two major chords are found.

The minor chords in every major key are found on the second, third, and sixth scale degrees of the major scale.

Section 2- *Song Structure*

Song form, simply put makes your song playable to musicians and an audience to enjoy. The lyrics and chords you have put together, must have an organized format.

You have listened to music, and you know there is a form and structure to the songs you have listened too but may not know what it is. This section is going to help you know how to get your song in a playable format, just like the songs you have heard.

A song has elements that are essential to making it playable and enjoyable to hear, without them the lyrics you have put chords too, sound chaotic and not organized. Many of you may know about what I am going to explain now, but I have no way of knowing those that don't, so, I am starting from the beginning for those who need it.

The first thing a song needs is a time signature. A time signature sets in motion how the song is structured into measures so it can be counted correctly. A song has measures of time for durations of chords and melody to be played. The time signature sets the parameters for how those measures are counted.

Counting is very important in music, and that cannot be stressed enough! You must be able to count the measures of a song with the correct time signature as you are structuring your song. Without the ability to count measures, you will never be able to format your song correctly, and musicians will not be able to accompany you as you play and sing!

Not only do you have to count measures of time, but you must do it evenly. This is called even tempo. Tempo is the speed of the count. If you count (1 2 3 4) for twelve sets with each one at different speeds, it will be difficult for someone to listen too and follow along if they are playing with you. So, the count of each measure must be even.

The ability to format your song into a time signature is step one. Step two is putting the song you are writing into measures, that follow the time signature. Both these steps require you to be able to count the measures in the time signature evenly from one to the next.

If you have never counted measures, it may be difficult to do it evenly, without speeding up or slowing down. You may try counting to sets of four, and record your voice doing it for twelve sets. Listen to it and see if you did it evenly. If you were able to do it with each measure evenly or close, you have good tempo. A Metronome (device that keeps time) is very helpful, and it would be good to get one and use it, even if your tempo is good.

Note vales

The basic note vales are on the music staff above. The time signature is four/ four. It simply means the quarter note is counted with four counts to each measure. The first staff has six measures with the following: Quarter note and quarter note rest, half note and half note rest, whole note, and whole note rest. Each measure gets four counts.

The second staff is showing how the quarter note is divided into first an eight note, and eight note rest, illustrating two eighth notes still equal one count, with two parts to the count. The sixteenth note is another division of the quarter note, into four parts.

Learning to count these basic note values is very important, but you must count them evenly in time and tempo. Your melody notes and chords you strum can have these various note values. The tab (six lines below the staff) is showing you where the note C is on the fifth string, third fret. You could replace the note with just a chord and practice these note vales too.

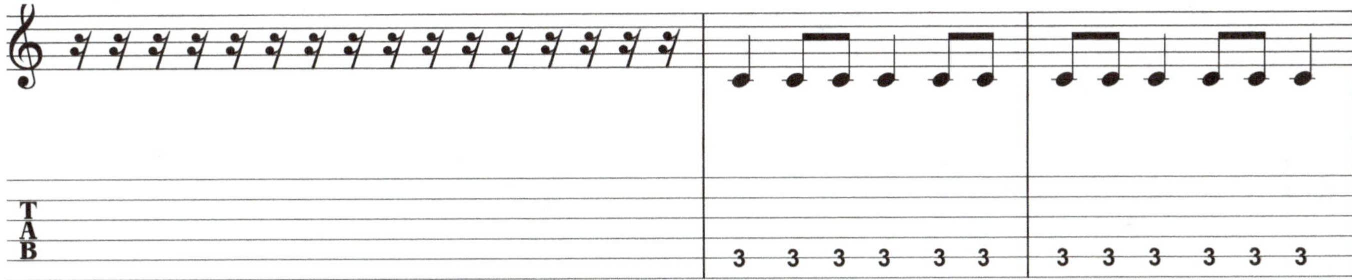

Counting Note Values

A measure can have multiple note values in it, and because of that it is difficult for those just learning to count to determine what note value a melody note has. The time signature governs all note values in each measure. The time signature of four/four is strictly to be adhered to, with each measure getting four counts. Once, you have learned to do that, your song will be easier to format with the number of measures, giving your song correct structure.

The melody of your song is a series of phrases, that can be counted using the time signature. This is where the various note values come into play. In a phrase a lyric is held out longer than others and vice versa. If a lyric gets two counts, or more or is faster than a previous one, you must be able to count it with the time signature.

Its very difficult to guide you in developing this ability without helping you in person, because I don't know what one reading this is, has for a particular melody. All I can do is give the mechanics involved to you and then its up to you to work it out.

With a metronome set at the speed (B P M) beats per minute which is the tempo of your song, then you must figure out what the note values are in the context of the time signature. The time signature for now is four/four. Practice playing the note values at B P M set on at very low speed and see if you can count each measure with four beats.

Applying Note Vales to Phrases

Applying note values to phrases is something that is endless. The syllables in words when it comes to artistic creativity has no rules as far as grammar goes. The melody is what controls the phrase, but the phrase needs to fit the time signature and tempo of the song.

The words " I love you", are in the example with several ways to phrase it with note values to give you an example of how each way stays within the time signature. Set the metronome up around 50- 60 B P M, and practice singing and saying those words with each measure. Then do the examples again but try to count in your head from one to four with each measure.

Don't forget to count the rests too, they are important to learn to count and feel. Not all phrase start on the first beat of the measure. You will learn that a lot songs use phrases that start on the second beat of the measure.

The word "you" is the subject and it's the most important word, so it should be a half note or a quarter note. But, it does not always follow this rule either, with important notes.

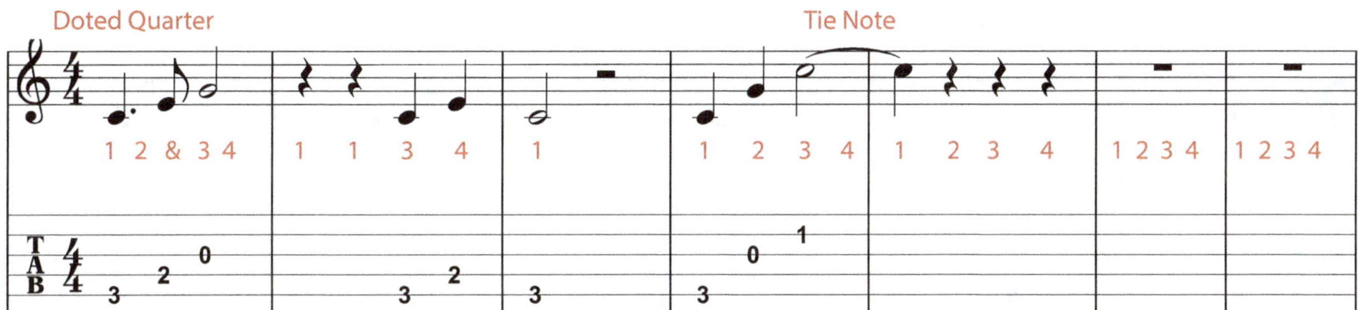

Applying Dotted and Tie Note Values

The note values in these examples are used for phrases that need longer durations of time than the ones you have learned so far. A dot added to a note extends that notes time duration by one half. The quarter note can be thought of as ringing for two eighth notes. So, a dotted quarter is counted as three eighth notes.

When a word that needs to last longer than a measure will allow, it can be tied to hang over into the following measure. The tie note is sounded only by the first note, the second note tied to the first note played, is meant to be sustained.

These phrases are examples of two bar (measure) phrases with the same words "I love you". The one bar phrases and now these two bar phrases give you some direction in learning to count measures with your lyrics.

Phrases can be several measures long. They can start anywhere in a measure as well. The most important thing to remember is to keep important words on the down beats (1 2 3 4) not subdivisions of those beats. Studying lyrics of songs that have been published that show how note values have been applied to those lyrics, is a great research project for you in developing the ability to structure your phrases.

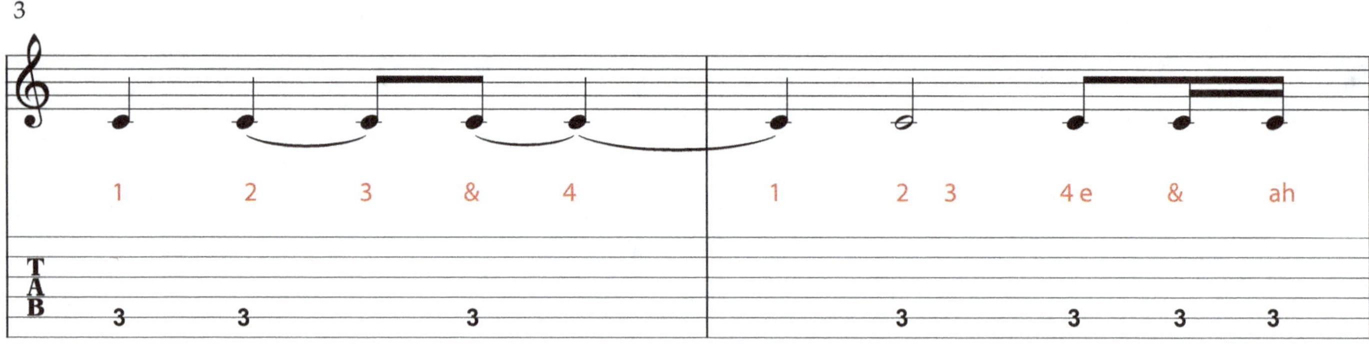

Applying Note Vales to Phrases

These Note values are more advanced than the previous ones you have learned. Most of the various note values you find in a lot of the songs you have heard will not be to much more then all of the ones you have learned.

The faster note values will be used with lyrics to more up tempo bouncy songs. Practice them with a metronome, until you can count them.

Look at a lot of songs with various note values, to learn more to help you structure your phrases into measures.

2/4	**Quarter Note gets one count**	**Beats per Measure**	**Two**
3/4	**Quarter Note gets one count**	**Beats Per Measure**	**Three**
5/4	**Quarter Note gets one count**	**Beats Per Measure**	**Five**
6/4	**Quarter Note gets one count**	**Beats Per Measure**	**Six**
7/4	**Quarter Note gets one count**	**Beats Per Measure**	**Seven**

2/8	**Eighth Note gets one count**	**Beats per Measure**	**Two**
3/8	**Eighth Note gets one count**	**Beats Per Measure**	**Three**
5/8	**Eighth Note gets one count**	**Beats Per Measure**	**Five**
6/8	**Eighth Note gets one count**	**Beats Per Measure**	**Six**
7/8	**Eighth Note gets one count**	**Beats Per Measure**	**Seven**

New Time Signatures

There are numerous time signatures, but in the realm of radio friendly air play only a few are used. The most popular one is four/four. Three/four is used a lot as well, but not as common as four/four. The more less used ones involve using the eighth note as the note that determines the count per measure.

Songs that use five/four and higher, are used more in jazz, fusion, jazz, and progressive rock. If you going to compose pop songs, you won't be using these time signatures.

Time signatures that use the eighth note as the denominator to count measures with, are in a lot of classical, and Baroque music. Some, blues songs and jazz too. But, in the realm of pop music, hardly ever.

The time signature's you use for your songs, is up to you to decide. Now, it is up to you to structure your lyrics into measures and phrases, and that is something that determines the time signature. The information you have in the last several Examples should help guide you.

As was mentioned before, the value of listening to songs and studying them for their time signatures and phrases cannot be stressed enough, in the help that will give you, for your songs.

Once, you have your time signature figured out, and measures for lyrics some-what mapped out, you need to structure the song. This involves verses, choruses, and other parts like a bridge, solos, introductions, and endings. For example, how many measures is the verse, or chorus, and other parts, are things you need to work out.

All that was just mentioned could not happen if you didn't have a time signature to base how the measures are counted. So, that's why giving you some direction on figuring out your time signature was required, to lead you to the next step. The next step is song Form!

Many song writers use set formulas such as verse, pre chorus, verse, pre chorus, chorus, followed by a bridge, then a chorus, and a third verse, pre chorus, chorus, and outro. There are many variations, such as two verses, then pre chorus, and chorus, and so forth. The song form you choose is up to you and is where you can be as creative as you want. Only thing you must keep in mind is, how will the form of your song be perceived by others, if you are wanting to gain wide commercial appeal!

Song writers use letters to label the parts of songs like, the letter A for the verse, B for the chorus, C for the bridge. So, a song form might be (A B A). this would be a simple form, of verse, chorus, verse. The song form (A A B A), would be two verses then a chorus. The song form, (A A B C), means two verses, chorus, bridge, then back to the A section and B section.

Within each section, there are norms for how many measures a section is. But the overall sections combined equal a standard number's for all too. For example, sixteen measures of verse, (A) section, then eight measures of chorus (B) section, is twenty-four measures for one loop, before it is all repeated. This would give you one loop that is twenty-four measures, and if you double it, you have forty-eight measures.

If you have two sixteen bar A sections, before the chorus, that would be a thirty-two bar(A A) section. The B section of eight bars, now makes a forty-bar loop. Thinking of song writing in loops, simplifies the process. If the A section is one loop, and the B section is another loop, you have two loops, that are repeated that is most of your song. When you combined those loops, you have a form Like, (A B A B), (A A B A B), and so on.

Most songs use numbers that are four, six, eight, twelve, sixteen, twenty-four, and thirty-two, bars four sections, and loops. The higher numbers will be for verses and choruses, lower numbers for intros and outros.

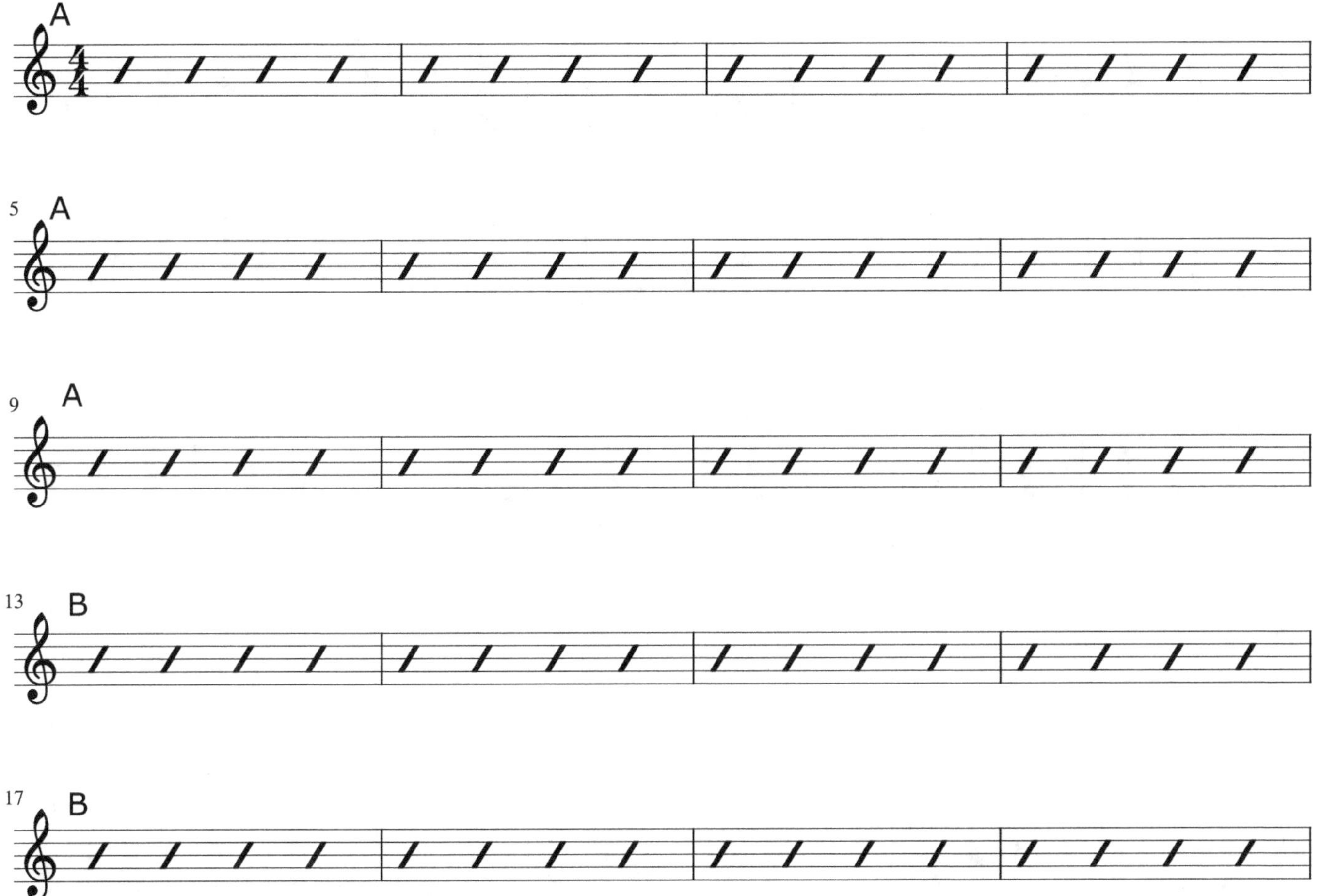

Organizing Your Thoughts

Getting organized in your thought process, helps to build your confidence that you will finish your song. You have direction, to aim your creativity towards. So, you are not sitting down to write with no goals, and objectives to reach. Mapping out the sections, gives you something to look at as you start to structure the phrases for each measure. The example above is how you would map out the A and B sections of a twenty-four bar loop.

The A section is twelve bars, and the B section is eight. Now, almost the entire song is mapped out, because you are going to repeat sections. Once you compose the A section, its going to be repeated and the same with the B section. Then the entire loop will be repeated, which is a large part of the song.

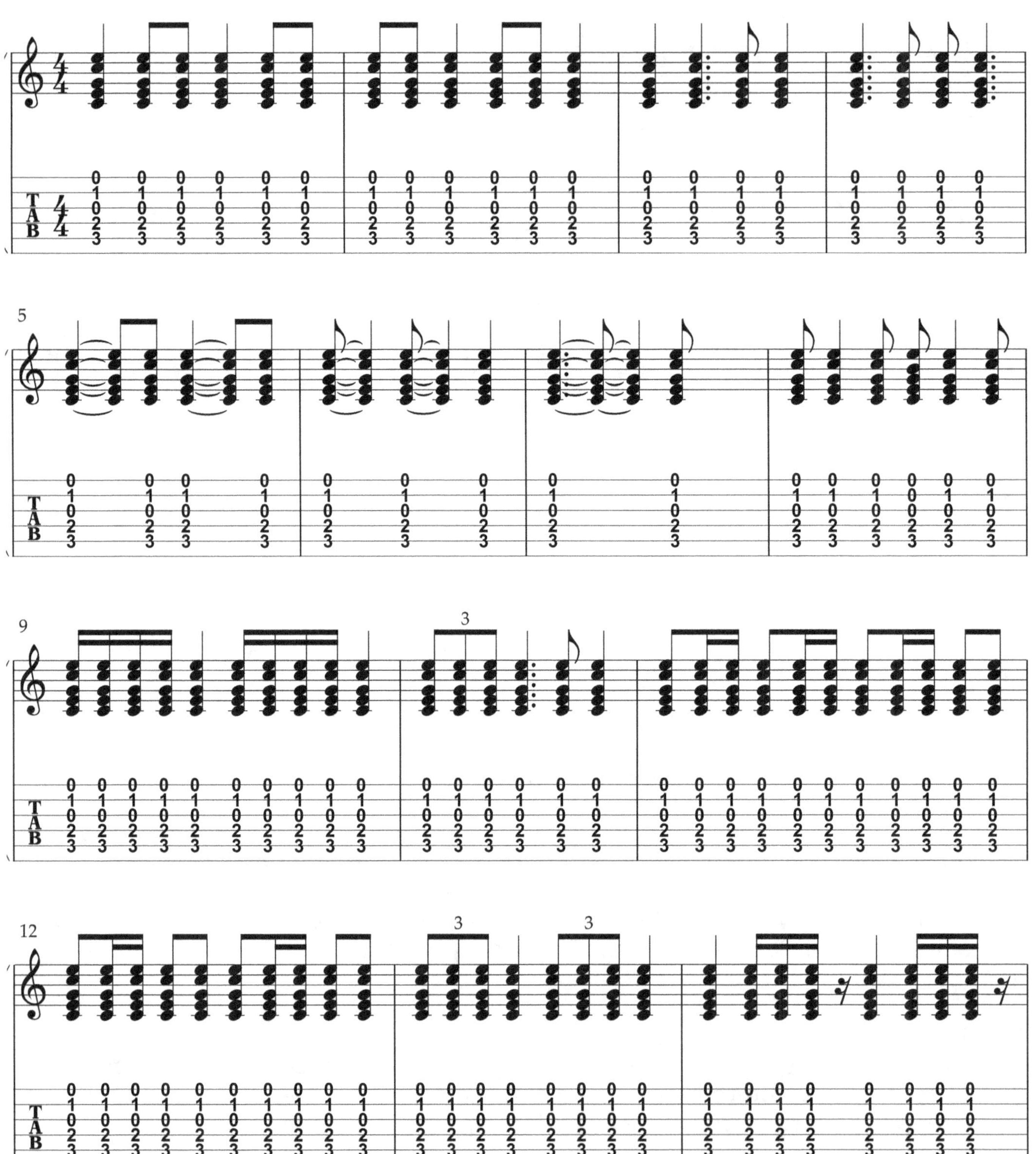

Writing Songs is a process that has a lot of steps if you are going to take your lyrics, and format them into a form that becomes a complete song. The purpose of this book is help guide you in how to take your lyrics and put chords and structure to them. At the same time with helping, you with song writing, this is also a book to help you become a better guitarist, as you compose. The guitar is the instrument you are composing with, so the more you learn about the guitar the better your compositions will be.

Up to this point, you have learned what keys are, and how to determine a key. The knowledge of keys, and the chords in keys, should give you confidence in choosing chords for your lyrics. This section was designed to help you get closer to putting your songs into a time signature, and form. There will be more lessons to come on song form, but you should start to practice putting some of your lyrics to what you have learned so far.

To begin with take your melodies, and use the lessons in determine what key you are in. Then you need to try to put your song into a time signature. This must be done before you can structure the measures, for verses, and choruses.

This section gave you some help and direction in putting note values to your melodies. This is a process that you need to work out. The note values will be difficult to do for you at first and frustrating. Eventually you will get good enough, to get a general idea, to accomplish what you need to do. Listening to artists, with some idea of what various note values are, now, will help you determine what a lot of them are. Using a metronome, is very important, in developing the ability to count steady beats.

Song form is up to you as to how many measures for choruses and verses, or adding a bridge, or solos, this is what your song form will consist of. You have the knowledge to achieve what has been covered so far, its just going to take time, and patience.

There are some rhythms to practice, chords, and loops, with but there is so much more to know. Listening to music and looking at professionally published books, of songs, will be a tremendous help too.

Song Form

Song From has covered first an introduction to song form. Song forms (A B A), (A A B A), (A B A C). The letters represent, Verses, choruses, bridges, and other parts of songs. The parts of songs are labeled this way to help song writers, organized, verses, choruses, bridges, and other parts. Its also how musicians think of song parts when their learning songs.

Measures, in song parts follow patterns involving set numbers, and several options, was covered. This helps you in the song organizing process.

Time Signatures

Time signatures are how songs are organized into measures, of time. Time signatures are needed to put songs into various forms and how melodies are structured into measures. Section two gave you some, insight in how to do that by reading and understanding note values. Several examples of various time signatures other than four/four time, were given in a table, to use with your song writing.

Mapping out songs

Mapping out songs was touched on to help you organize the thought process, in your song writing.

Rhythms

Example of rhythms were given to put to chords that will give you some direction for how to play various beats and rhythms in your song writing.

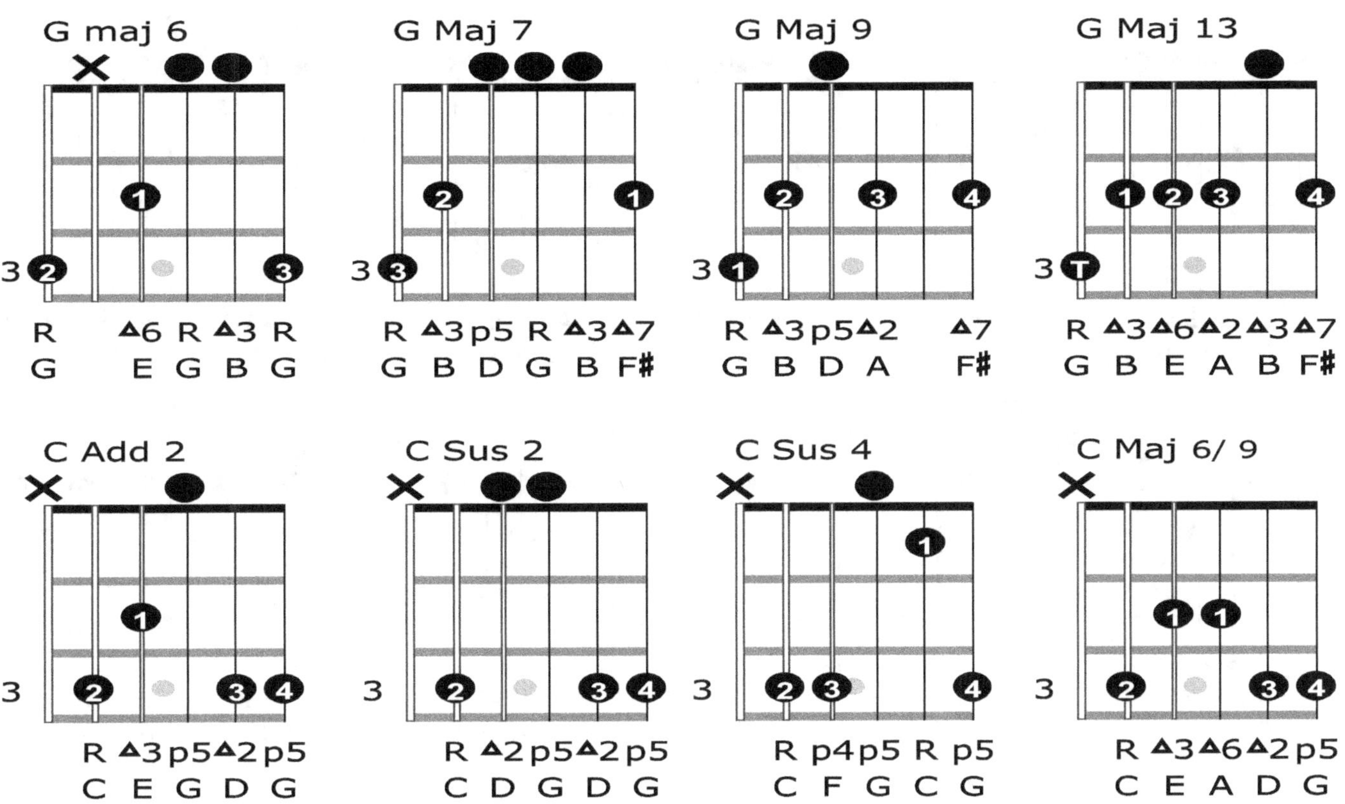

Major 6th	Major 7th	Major 9th	Major 13 th
1 3 5 6	1 3 5 7	1 3 5 7 9	1 3 5 7 9 13 (6)
1 3 5 6	1 3 5 7	(5) can be omitted	(5) (9) can be omitted

Add 2 (9)	Sus 2	Sus 4	Major 6 9
1 3 5 2	1 2 5	1 5 4	1 3 5 6 9

Chord Extensions Explained

A triad is the foundation that extensions are added. The tables explain the various ways to add notes to all major triads. You can omit the fifth of the chord if needed. The seventh of the chord must be included in the major nine and thirteenth chord. The ninth can be omitted in the major thirteenth.

The minor chord extensions will just have a lowered third and lowered seventh. The seventh chord, will have a lowered seventh, but the major third.

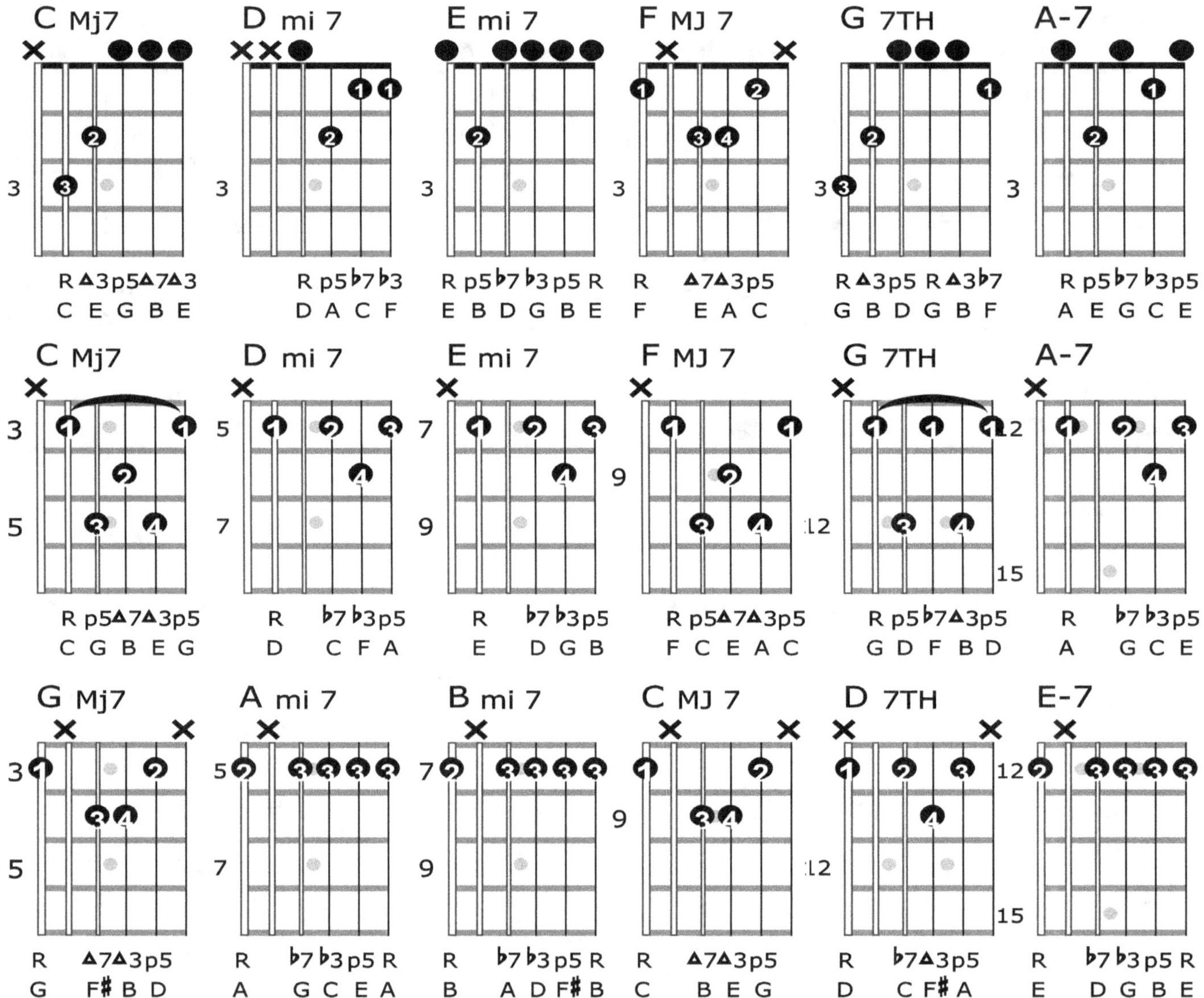

1 maj 7	2 mi 7	3 mi 7	4 maj 7	5 7th	6 mi 7	7 mi 7 b5
1 3 5 7	1 b3 5 b7	1 b3 5 b7	1 3 5 7	1 3 5 b7	1 3 5 b7	1 b3 b5 b7

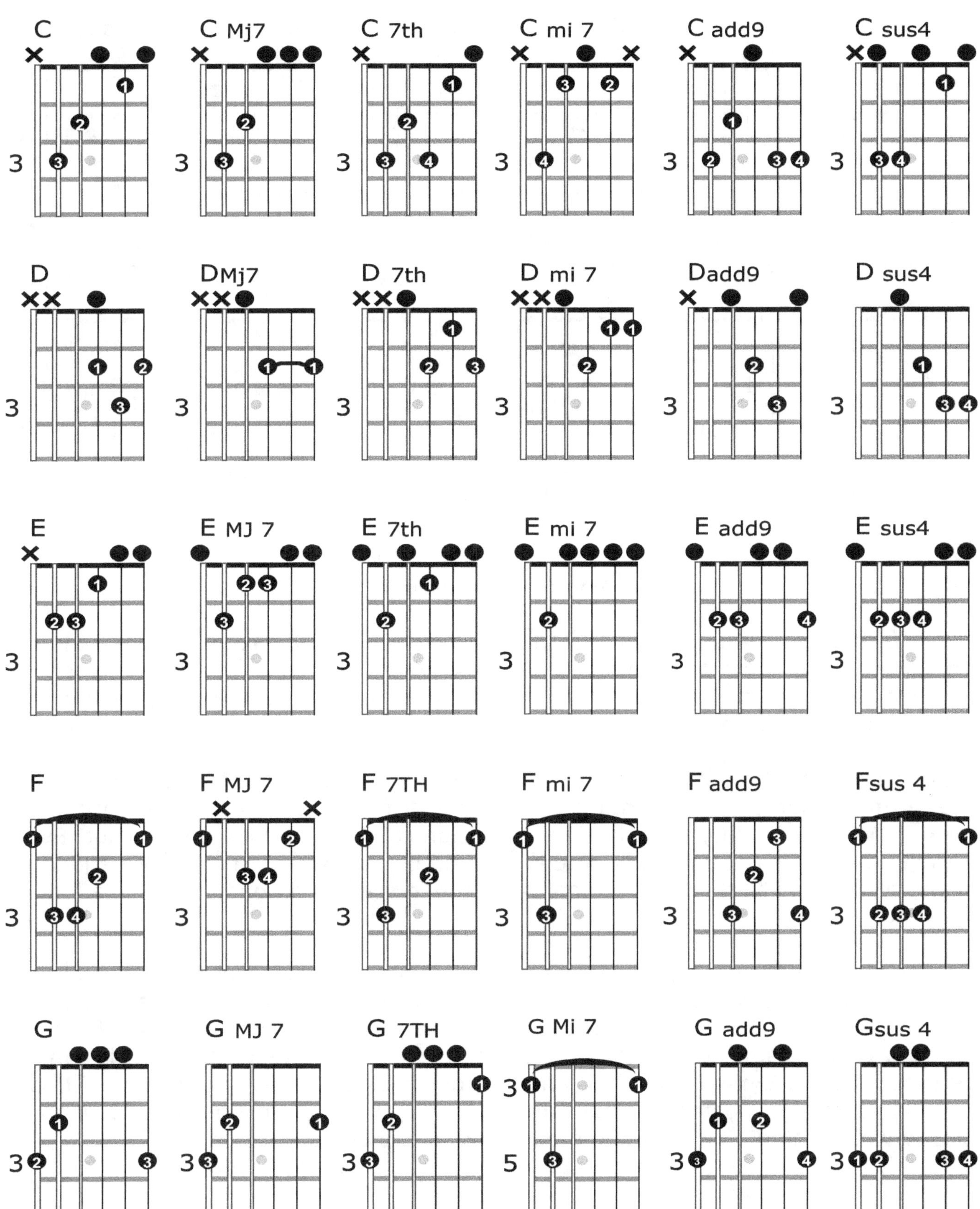

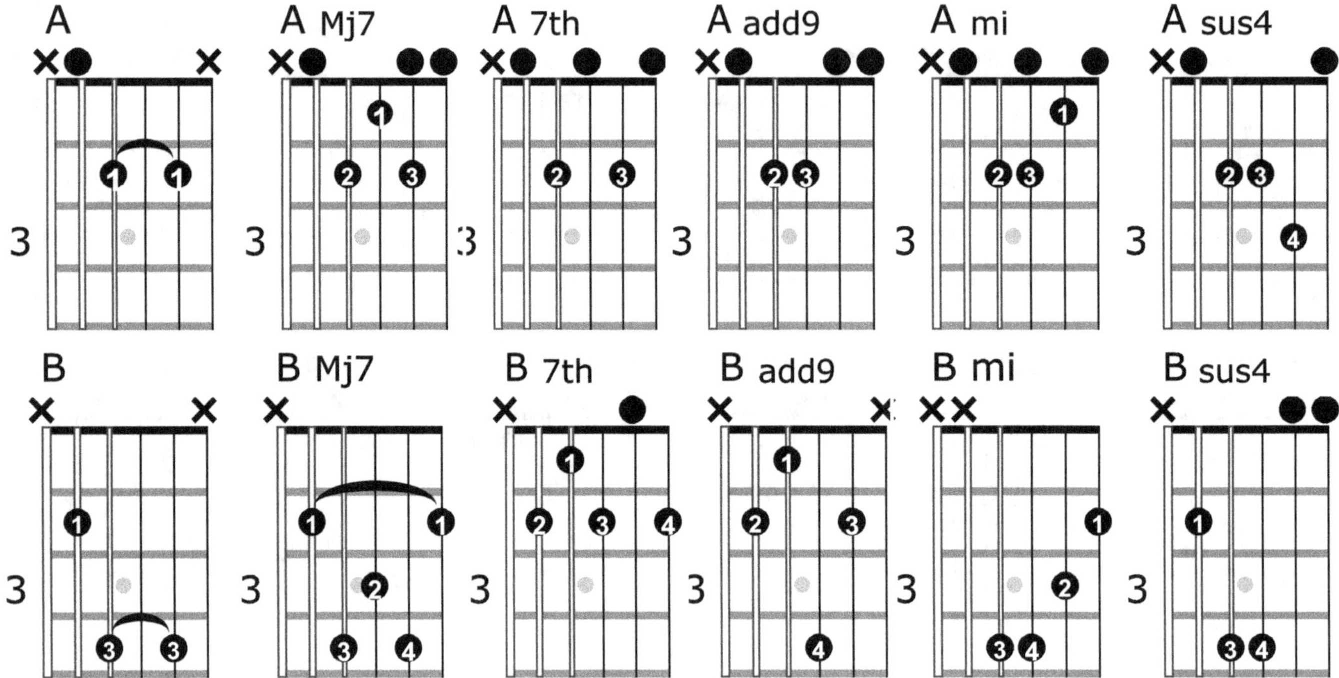

Applying Chord Extensions

It will take a few years to build a good knowledge base of chords. All these chords are here to give you a point of reference as a song writer. You will find by experimenting with chords over your melodies and lyrics, chord extensions can add new dimensions to your songs.

Major chords stay major and minor chords remain minor as well as you apply the use of these chords in your writing. For a C major chord use C major seventh or for A minor use A minor seventh. The extension can be a melody note or not. Even if the extension is not a melody note the sound of the extensions that are added to the triads, create chord movement rather than staying on one chord for a long duration.

Chord extensions can get into the area of chord substitutions too. For example, C major seventh can take the place of E minor. The notes of E minor are (E G B), the notes of C major seventh are (C E G B). The notes of A minor are (A C E), the notes of F major seventh are (F A C E). Both major seventh chords C and F, can be thought of as E minor over a C, and A minor over an F. The relationship of this rule is this, the root notes a major third up from any major seventh chord, when played with a minor chord can be thought of as explained.

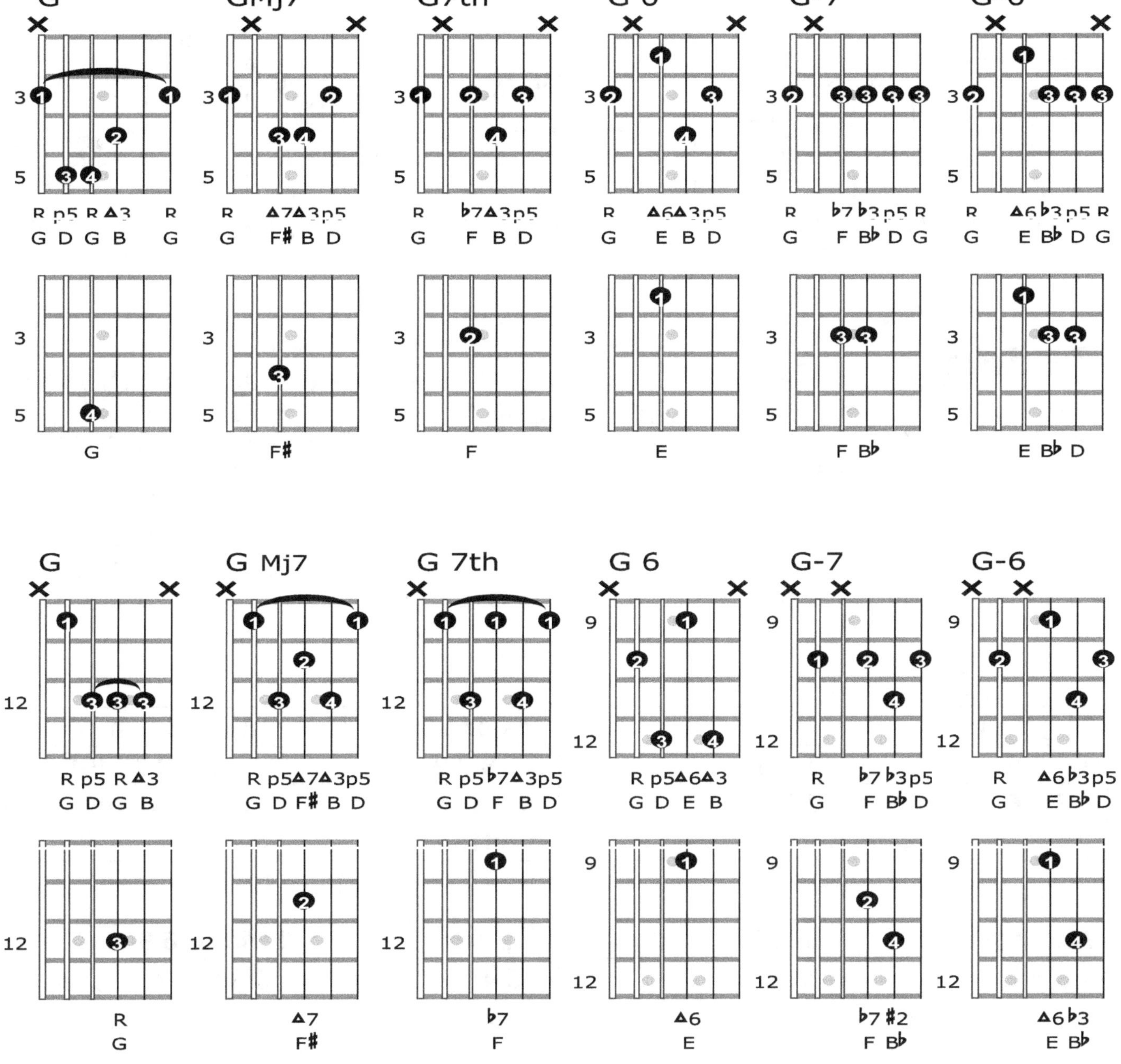

Tips for Memorizing Chords

The second row below each group of chords is illustrating how to memorize these chords and all chords. It highlights the root, moving half steps down to form first, major seventh, then dominant seventh, and major sixth chords. The third and fifth of the chord never change.

For minor chords the root and fifth remain the same, the third is lowered a half step, and the seventh is lowered too.

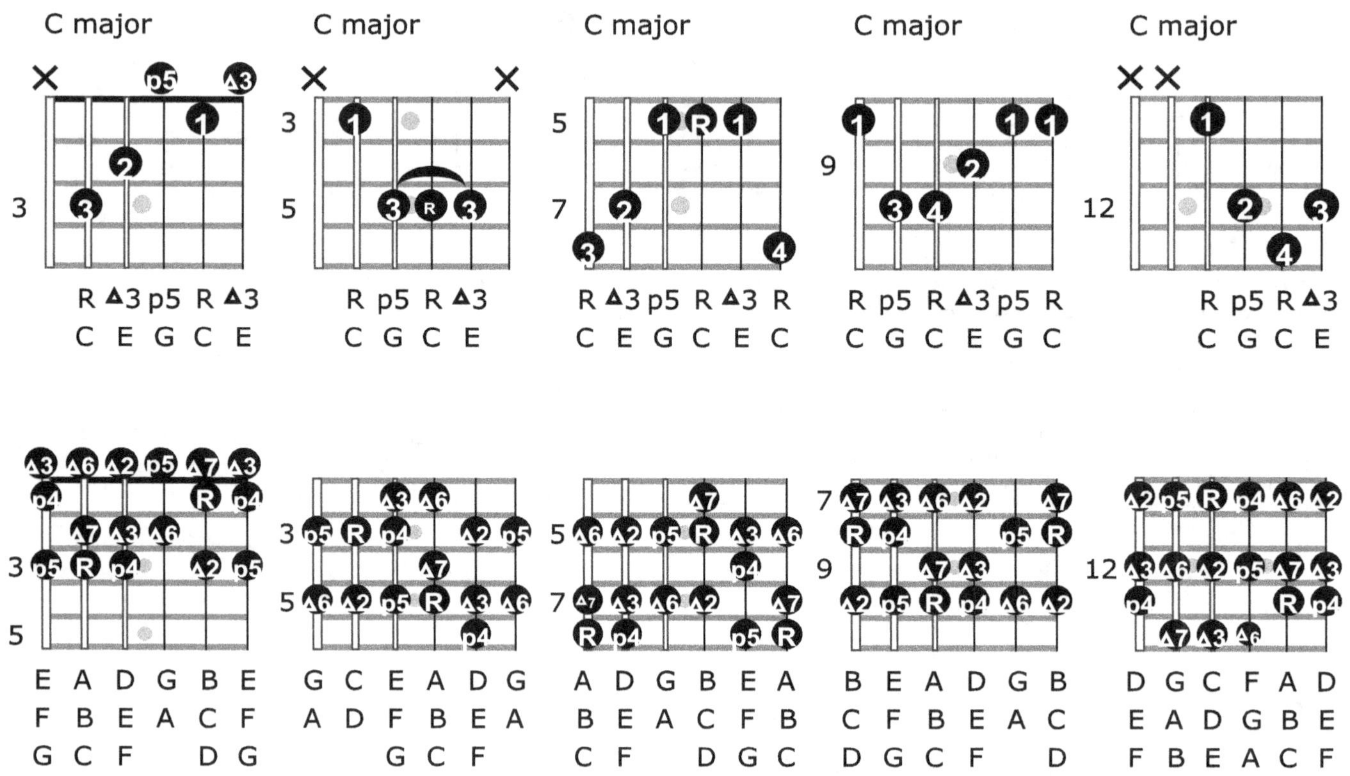

Major 6th	Major 7th	Major 9th	Major 13 th
1 3 5 6	1 3 5 7	1 3 5 7 9	1 3 5 7 9 13 (6)
1 3 5 6	1 3 5 7	(5) can be omitted	(5) (9) can be omitted

Add 2 (9)	Sus 2	Sus 4	Major 6 9
1 3 5 2	1 2 5	1 5 4	1 3 5 6 9

Using the Five Shapes to Build Chords

Once, you know and understand chord formulas, all chords can be built from the five basic scale grouping of notes here for C major. The top row is the basic major triad. From that triad shape, use the scale below to add the extensions.

For minor chords lower the third and seventh. For seventh chords lower just the seventh.

G Mj7

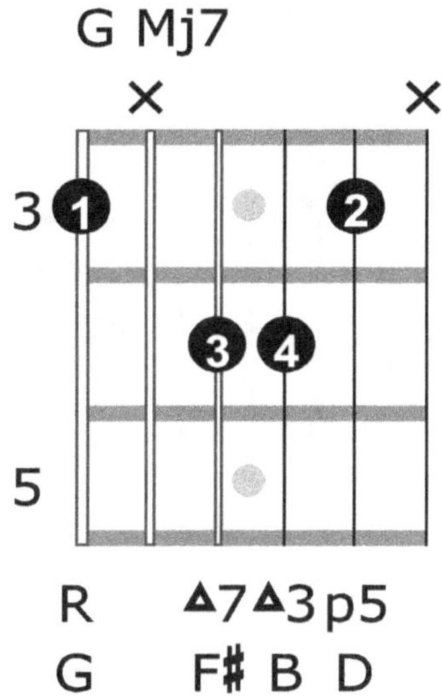

A -7

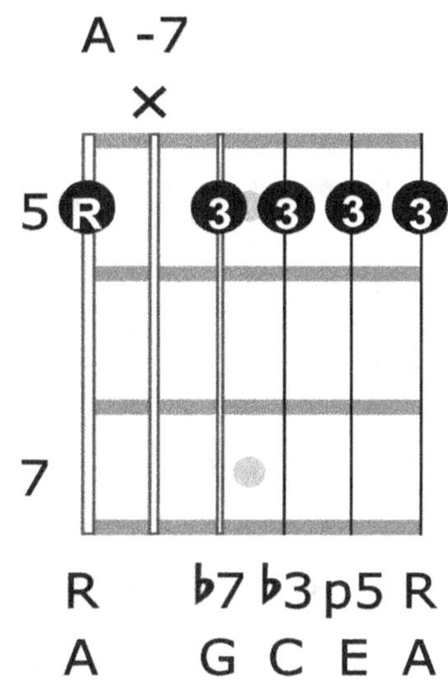

B -7

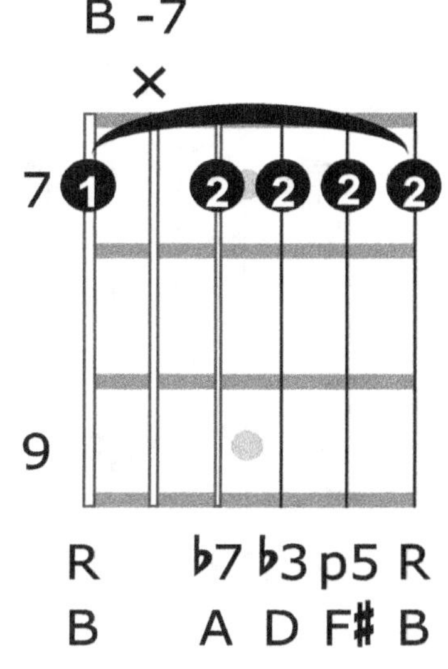

C Mj7

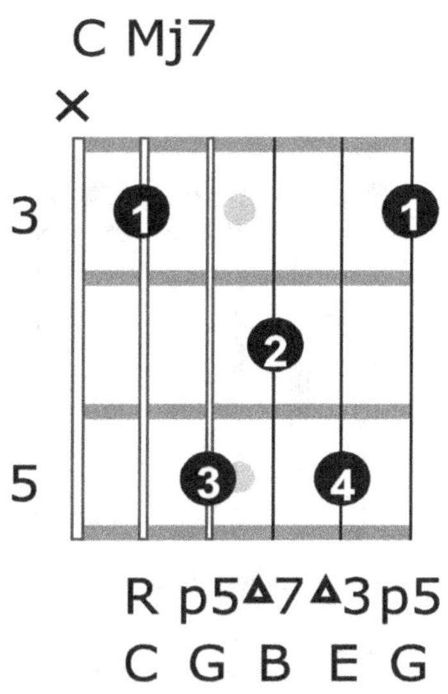

D 7th

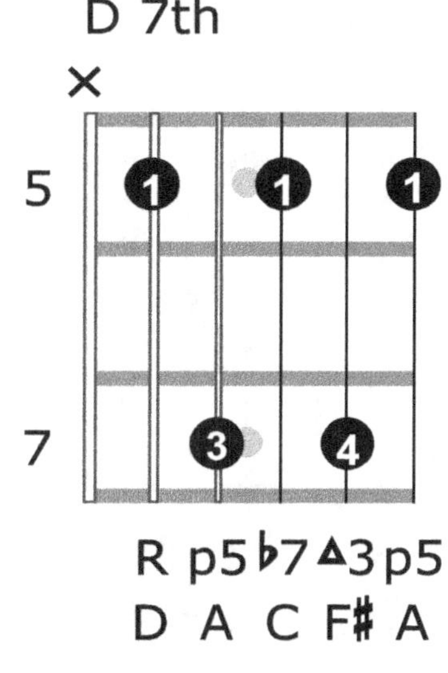

E -7

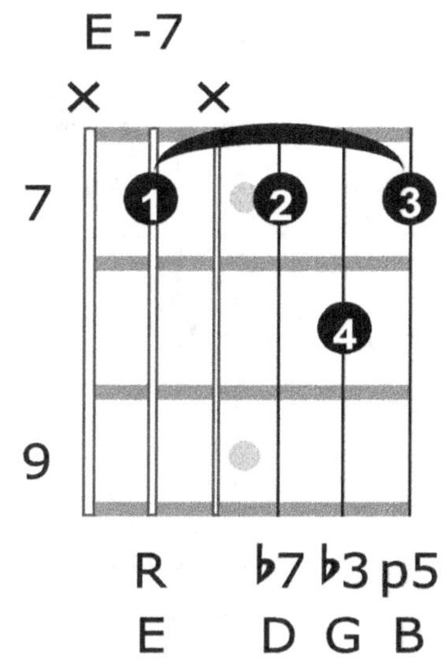

Chords 1- 6

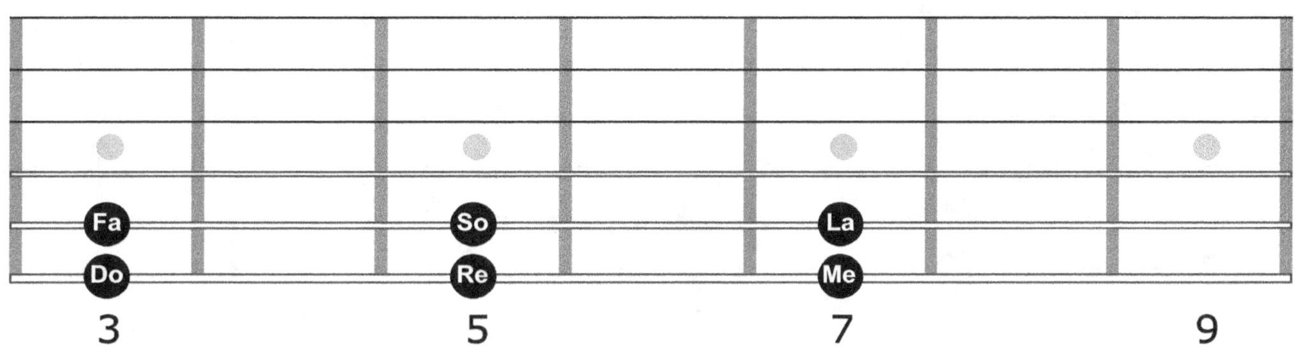

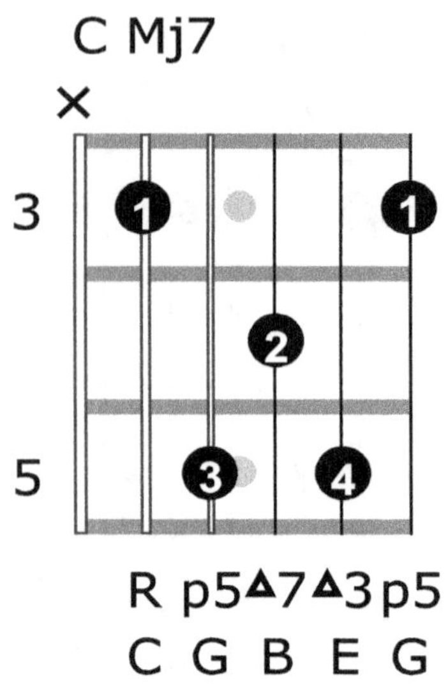

C Mj7

R p5△7△3 p5
C G B E G

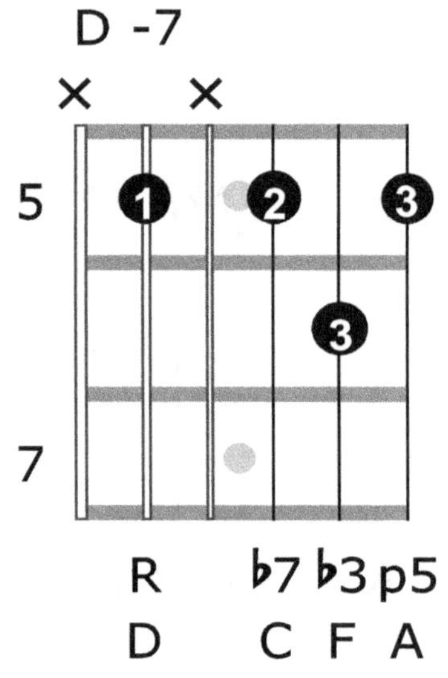

D -7

R ♭7 ♭3 p5
D C F A

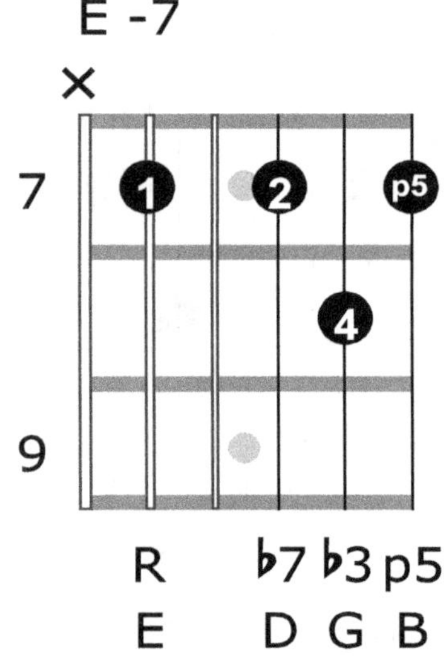

E -7

R ♭7 ♭3 p5
E D G B

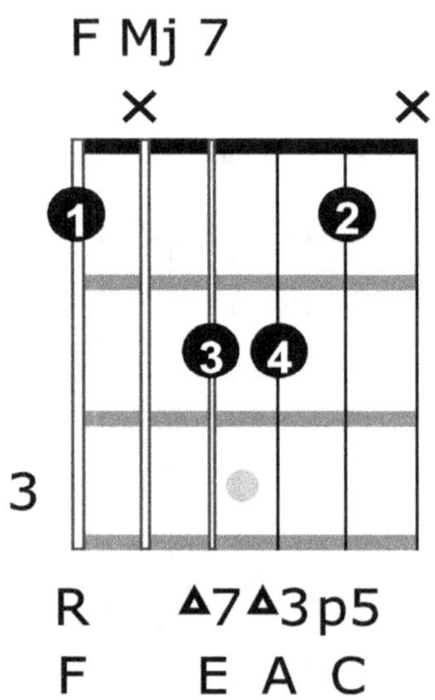

F Mj 7

R △7△3 p5
F E A C

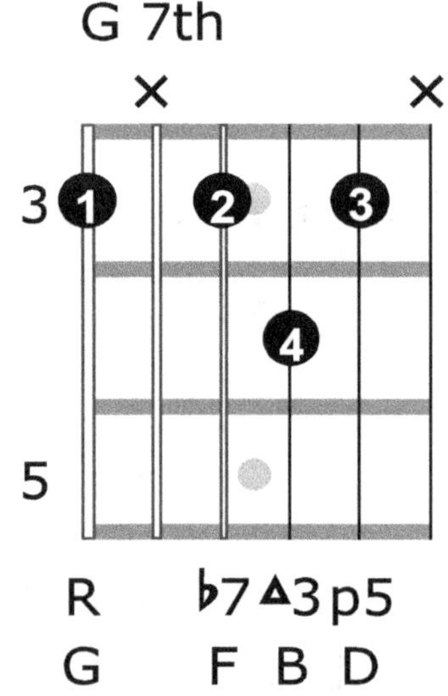

G 7th

R ♭7 △3 p5
G F B D

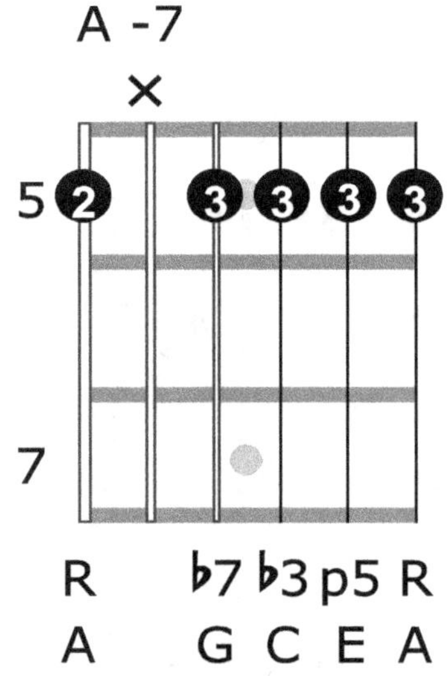

A -7

R ♭7 ♭3 p5 R
A G C E A

Chords 1- 6

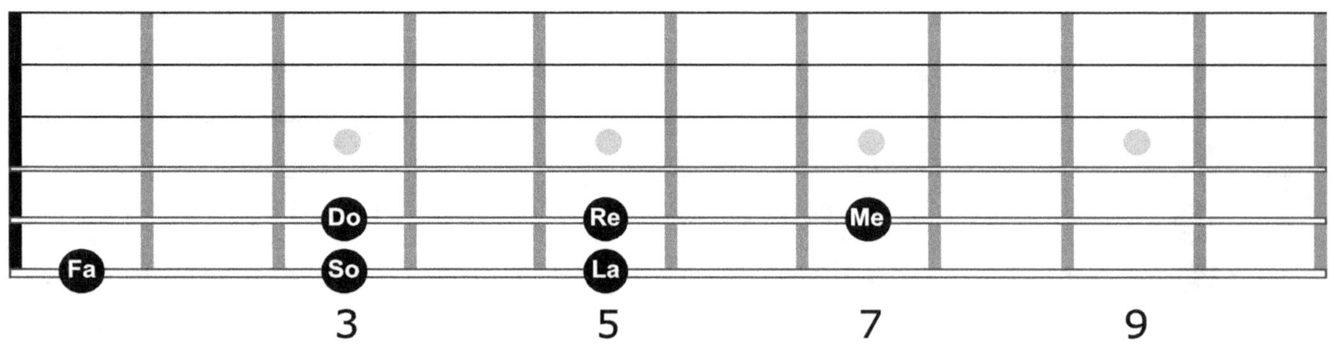

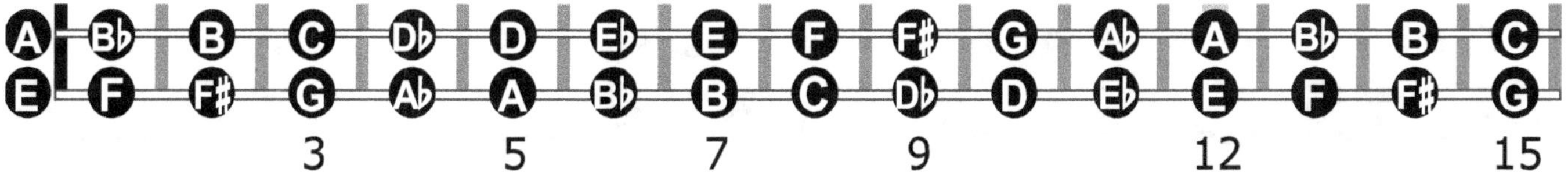

Sixth String Root Notes (Do Re Me)			Fifth String Root Notes (Fa So La)		
Do	Re	Me	Fa	So	La
C	D	E	F	G	A
G	A	B	C	D	E
D	E	F#	G	A	B
A	B	C#	D	E	F#
E	F#	G#	A	B	C#
B	C#	D#	E	F#	G#
F#	G#	A#	B	C#	D#
Db	Eb	F	Gb	Ab	Bb
Ab	Bb	C	Db	Eb	F
Eb	F	G	Ab	Bb	C
Bb	C	D	Eb	F	G
F	G	A	Bb	C	D

Fifth String Root Notes (Do Re Me)			Sixth String Root Notes (Fa So La)		
Do	Re	Me	Fa	So	La
C	D	E	F	G	A
G	A	B	C	D	E
D	E	F#	G	A	B
A	B	C#	D	E	F#
E	F#	G#	A	B	C#
B	C#	D#	E	F#	G#
F#	G#	A#	B	C#	D#
Db	Eb	F	Gb	Ab	Bb
Ab	Bb	C	Db	Eb	F
Eb	F	G	Ab	Bb	C
Bb	C	D	Eb	F	G
F	G	A	Bb	C	D

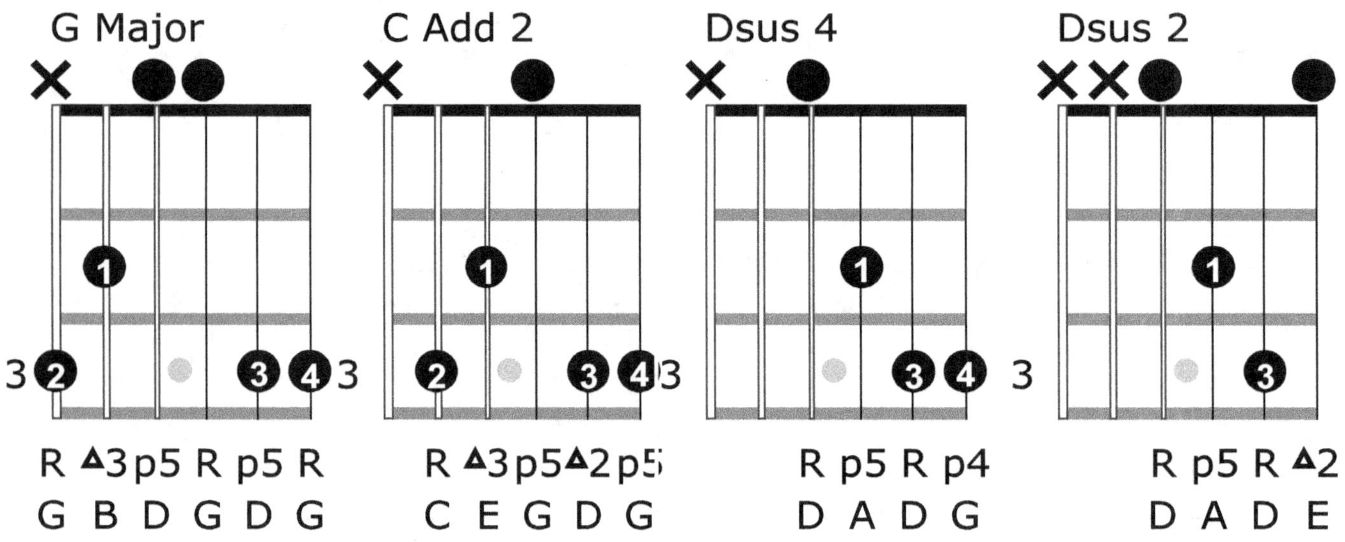

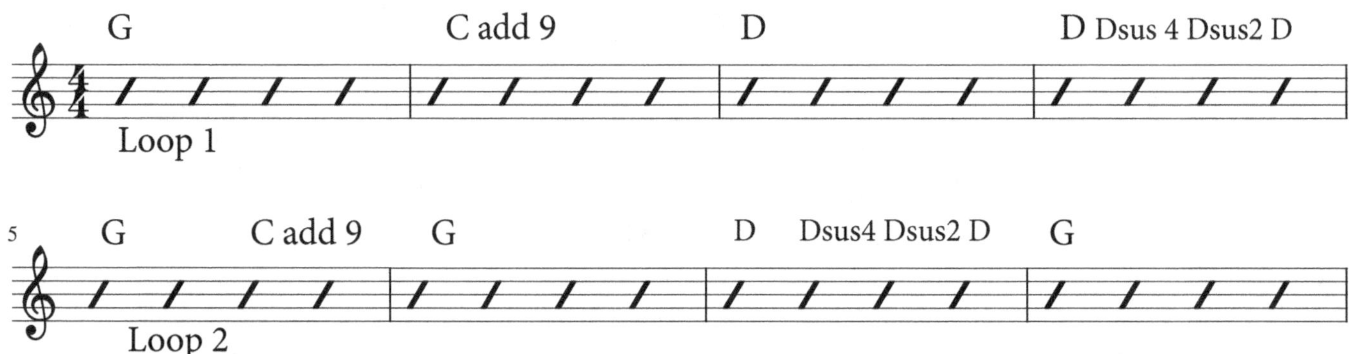

Chord Extensions in G

The chords above and loop below are found in many songs in the keys of G in the open position. The extra D in the G chord makes it easy to change to the C add 2 chord, and then the D chord and its extensions.

The capo is used often to move the open position so these chords can be played in any key a singer needs.

Chord Extensions

Adding notes to the triads create Chord extensions. Major 6, 7, 9, and 13 are possible. The same extensions can be added to the minor triad too. Add chords and Suspended chords are other ways to add notes to chords.

Building Chord Vocabulary

As a song writer you can be more creative if you know a lot of chords. So, building a good chord vocabulary is important. A lot of material was provided to help you start to do more than just use basic triads.

Chord Extensions and Chord Theory

Understanding how chords are constructed is important for several reasons, not only to help you learn them faster and more effectively, but to apply them to your songs, it helps to know the notes in the chords. This is why a lot of attention was given to chord theory and fretboard theory, to help guide you in learning chords as to where they are on your fretboard.

Using a Capo

The use of the capo has various purposes. Many song writers don't care to learn a lot about the guitar and just want to put basic chords to their songs, to get them to a place, to just sing over them. The capo allows a guitar player to move open position chords all over the guitar. There are lessons in section 2, to show how that is done. Another purpose for a capo is also illustrated with certain chords like the D suspended and add chords. These chords are easy to play in the open position, and used a lot in songs, with a capo they can be played in different fret locations.

The open position gives more freedom with chords due to open strings, that do not require fingers to play the notes that normally would use fingers. As the capo is moved around to various keys, it can be thought of as moving the open position. As a song writer you can play very creative chord backdrops with a capo.

Section 4- *Pop Music*

This section we will talk about pop music and our pop culture's musical history. You cannot begin to write pop songs without understanding the culture of pop music. Before any artist you hear today could enter the portals of pop music, the musical D N A had to be created that is the essence of pop music.

Before there was pop music there was serious music as it is called by those who want to be precise in the inclusion of the contributions from the great composers throughout history. We who are not as precise in labeling their works as serious, call it classical music. But how its thought of as it pertains to this discussion, matters not as far as what needs to be said.

The great composers forged their way through the mysteries of music yet to be unraveled in our evolution, musically speaking. They formed a lot of the structure that is in all songs. But their contribution was only the start.

The pop culture of music we know today is a conglomerate of melodies, rhythms, and melodic themes, that has evolved from classical music, folk music jazz, rock metal, country, and forms of the mentioned, to fusion styles.

A pop artist you hear today, can draw from all the various musical back drops that are now in the realm of our culture. But, pop music, does have boundaries that confine it to what is acceptable to most of the mainstream airways. It cannot be dated, the same old same old heard over and over. Something new must be in the mix to relate to the listener, and consumer of pop music. This is what producers do, they listen to an artist to see if there is that something new.

The world of pop music is defined by those who buy the songs and go to the concerts and shows. This is how it has been from the start of pop music. Because of this truth, music that is mainstream pop, is not serious (classical) musical, blues, jazz, heavy metal, or fusion styles of music. Pop music can be rock, country, and hip hop because the masses don't really appreciate serious and more musically involved forms of music, theoretically and technically speaking. You can draw ideas from the forms of music that is not pop, but the feel you put them in has to remain in a category more simple and easy listening music.

So, if you want to be a pop artist as a song writer you will have to follow the trends of pop music. What is popular today is mostly music I am personally not into, because I do like the more serious and technically involved music. But I do know a lot of the elements of pop music, from being a musician.

The information I am sharing here is strictly to be used as guide for writing pop music. Stay away from heavy metal, blues, jazz, and fusion styles. Write music that is easy to listen too, not too involved in a lot of changes, that are tempo and time signature changes. The average listener of pop music wants a good melody, and a nice beat, slow or fast, as long as it is consistent.

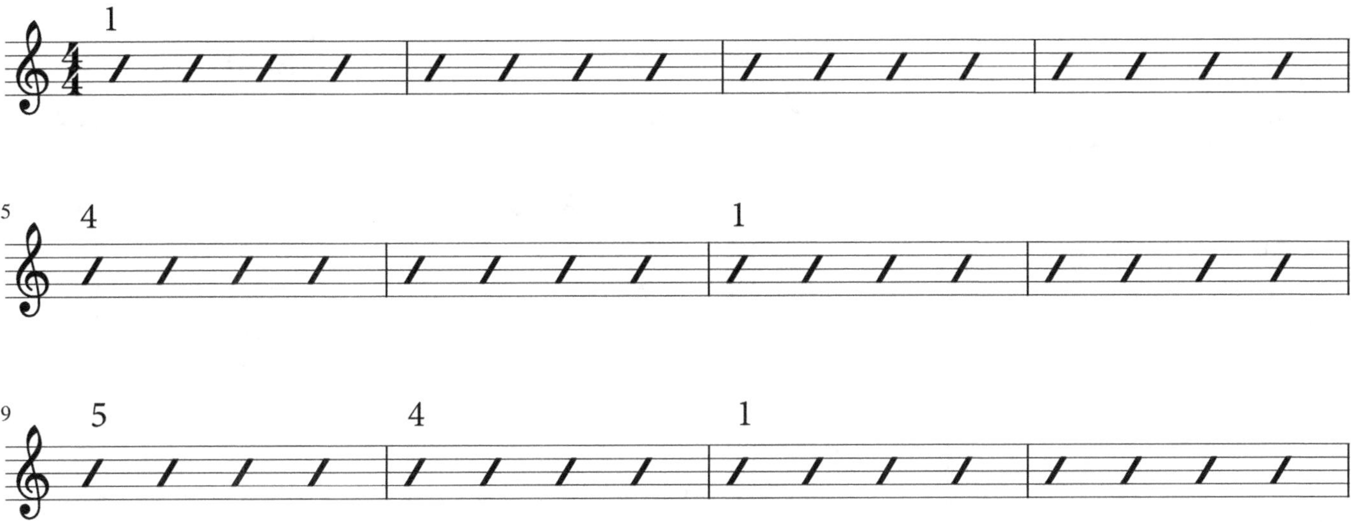

One chord	Four chord	Five chord
C Seventh	F Seventh	G Seventh
G seventh	C seventh	D seventh
D seventh	G seventh	A seventh
A seventh	D seventh	E seventh
E seventh	A seventh	B seventh

Twelve Bar Blues

The Twelve bar blues is perhaps the earliest form of pop song structure and form where blues rock and rock music emerged from. The blues form is found in so many forms of music, and because of that it will be used to form the foundation of pop music.

In its basic structure it is three seventh chords as the chart above is showing for five keys for root notes that are not diatonic. This form was once very popular and in some circles of musicians it is mostly what they play even today. A lot of easy songs can be written with the twelve bar blues form.

Even if you do not want to play blues it should be studied because a lot of song structure is based from the blues.

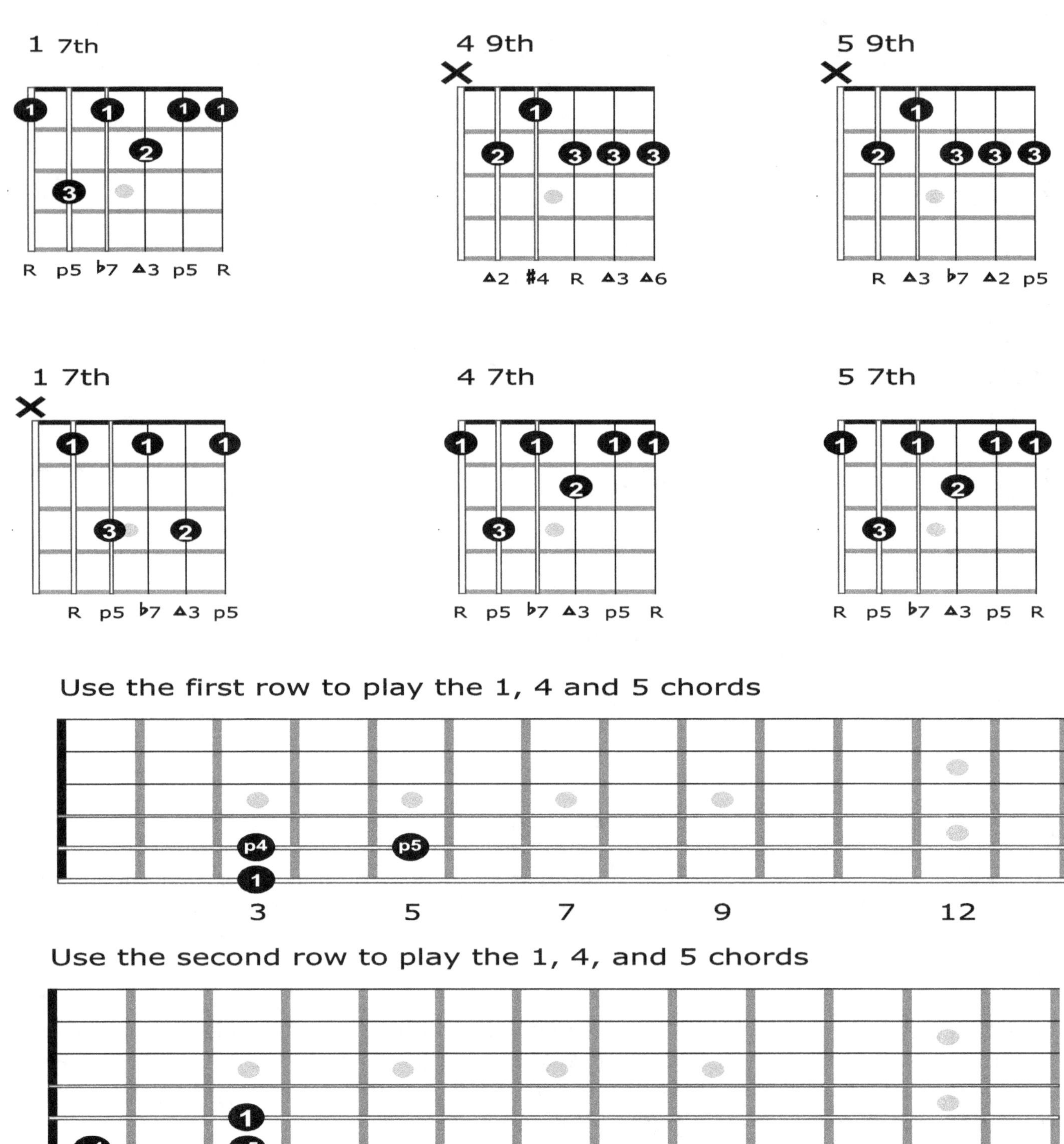
1 7th
R p5 b7 ▲3 p5 R

4 9th
▲2 #4 R ▲3 ▲6

5 9th
R ▲3 b7 ▲2 p5

1 7th
R p5 b7 ▲3 p5

4 7th
R p5 b7 ▲3 p5 R

5 7th
R p5 b7 ▲3 p5 R

Use the first row to play the 1, 4 and 5 chords
p4 p5 1
3   5   7   9   12

Use the second row to play the 1, 4, and 5 chords
p4 p5 1
3   5   7   9   12

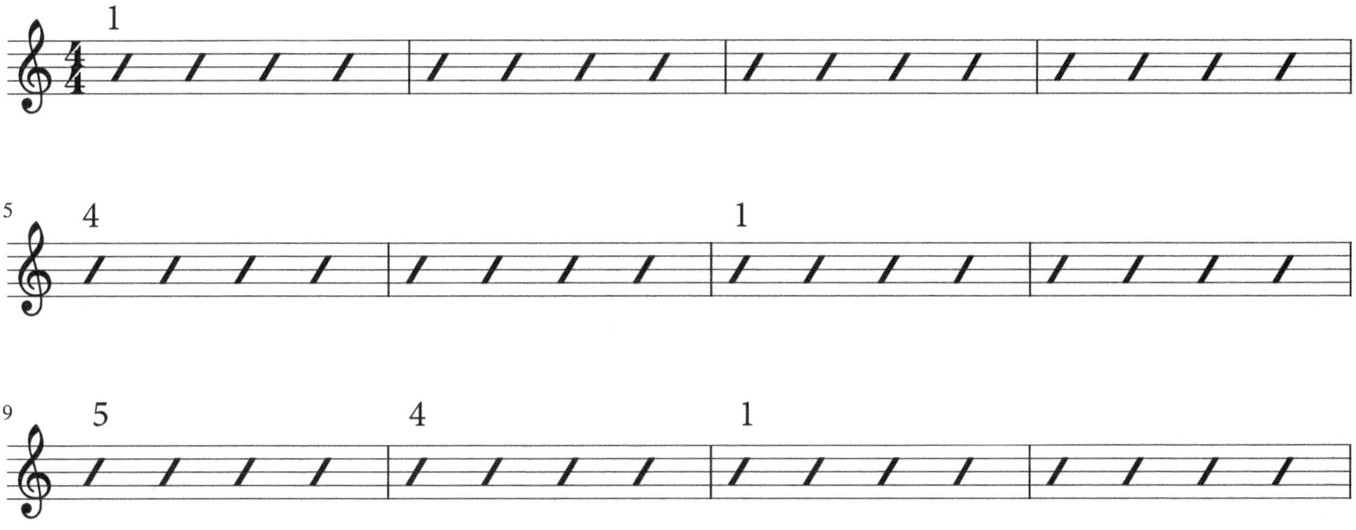

	Two	Three	Four	Five	Six	Seven
Root - 1						
C E G	D F A	E G B	F A C	G B D	A C E	B D F
G B D	A C E	B D F#	C E G	D F# A	E G B	F# A C
D F# A	E G B	F# A C	G B D	A C# E	B D F#	C# E G
A C# E	B D F#	C# E G#	D F# A	E G# B	F# A C#	G# B D

Root- One chord	Four chord	Five chord
Three and Six	Two and Six	Two, and Seven

Understanding Chord Function

Using the 12 bar Blues form for pop song forms with the one four and five chords and converting it back to a major key is going to be where you will start to build song structure from. The one chord can use the three and six chord's as substitute chords. Compare the notes of the C chord with the notes of the E minor and A minor chords. You will notice they both have two common notes with the C chord.

Compare the notes of the F chord with the D minor and A minor chords and you will see they have two notes in common too.

Last compare the notes of the D minor chord and the triad starting on B and you will see they have two common notes in them with the G chord. So we can break all seven chords down to the one four and five chords as far as function is concerned.

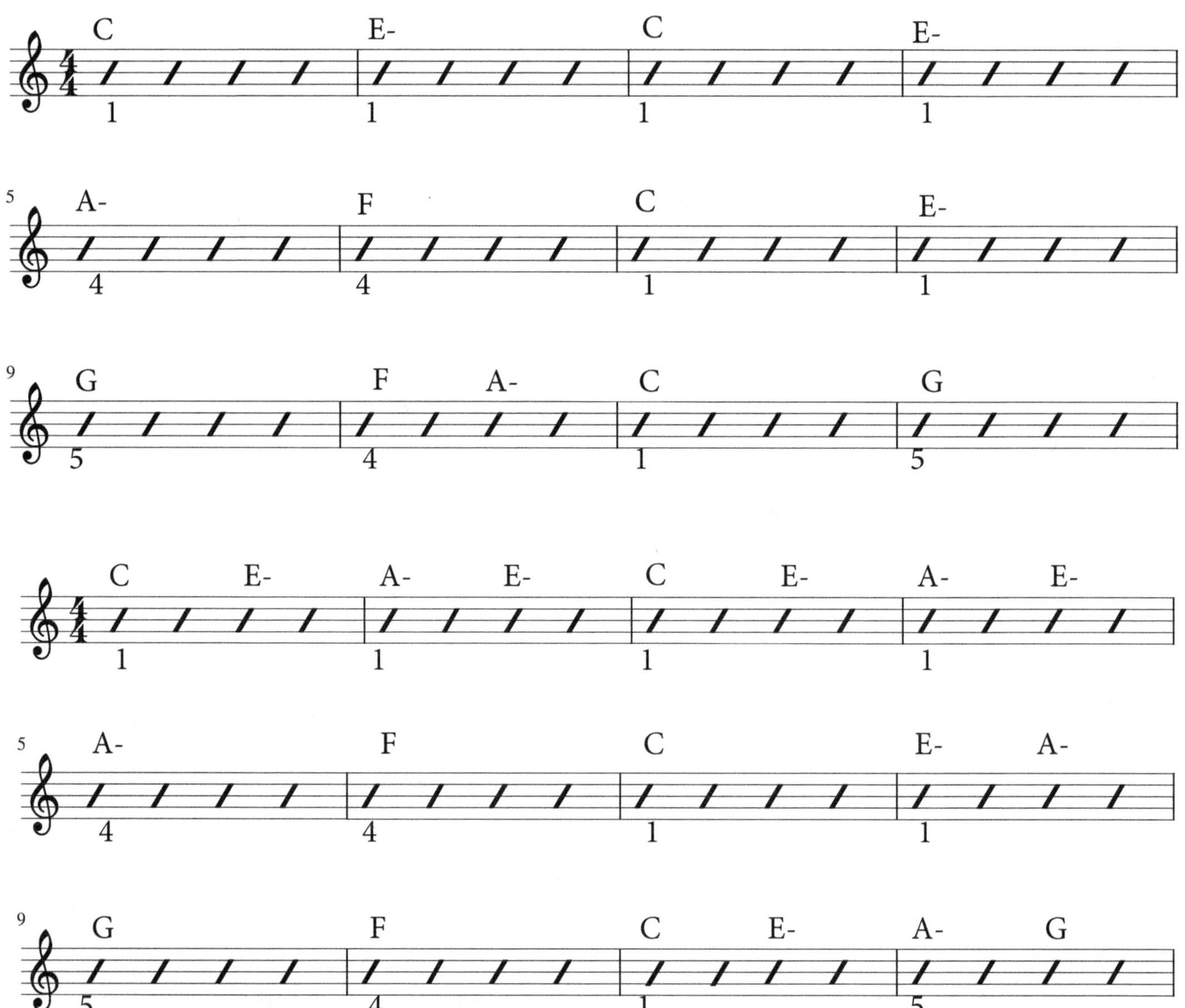

Converting the Twelve Bar Blues

The 12 bar structure has now been converted to a pop form. Both examples keep the chord functions in place except for the last measure in the second example has a G chord. This is to give the progression a feeling of ending of the first 12 bars with the use of the five chord as a five one Cadence, (the end of a phrase).

Now you have a possible 24 bar form if you repeated it for a verse, verse form or A A.

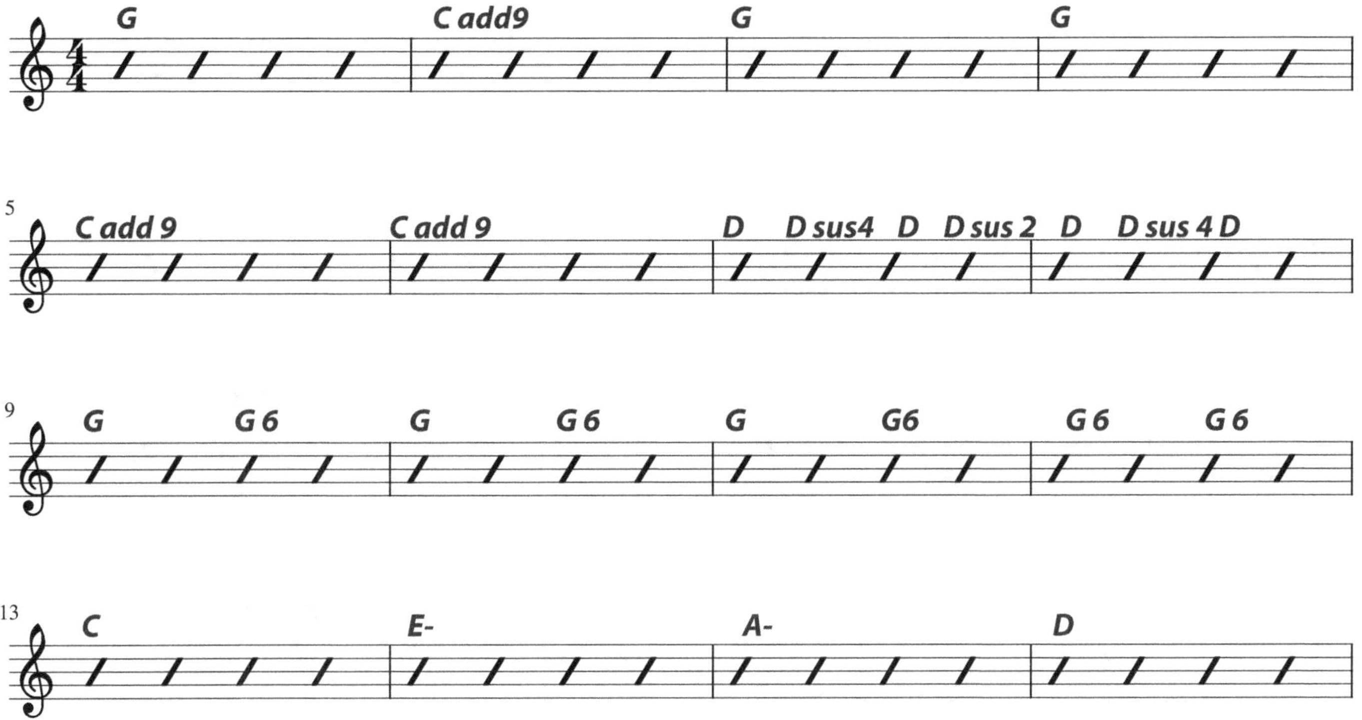

The Eight and Sixteen Bar Verse

The twelve bar blues structure stays on the one chord and four chords in four bars for the one cord only then two bars of the four chord. Or it has one bar for the one chord and four chords each, followed by two bars of the one, and two bars of the four.

Using just the structure of the first 8 bars of the 12 bar Blues the 8-bar form for the verse is developed that is used for pop music. The first six measures stay on the one and four chord functions. The five chord takes place of the last two measures to lead back to the one chord for a five one cadence.

Many songs have eight bars for a verse then the chorus. This song structure is found in a lot of Beatles songs among many other artists as well. I recommend a study of many Beatle songs for further analysis.

The second eight bars stays on the one chord for four measures. It uses an alternate chord pattern of two beats for the one and two beats for the one major six chords. The last four measures stay on the four chord function with the use of minor chords.

This example could function as an eight bar verse or a sixteen bar verse, in the key of G major.

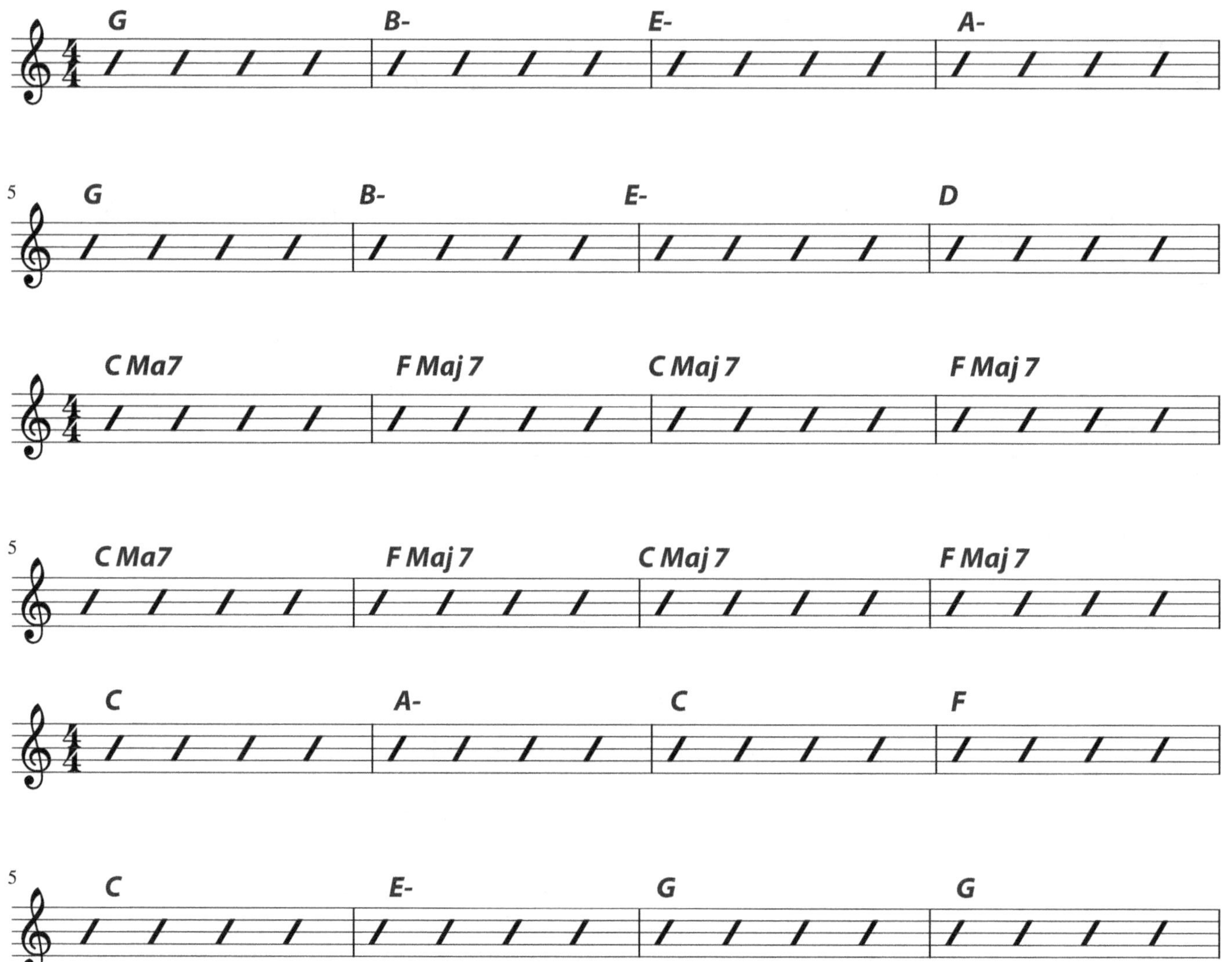

Using Song Form and Chord Function

The three examples of eight bar versus maintain the one and four functions for the six bars as before. These examples in creating progressions will serve as a guide to help you build 8 bar or 16 bar versus. You have guidelines you can follow to create with rather than approaching you're writing blindly. Keep in mind with all guidelines that you have for progressions the melody that you come up with is really the most important thing and the chords need to follow that melody.

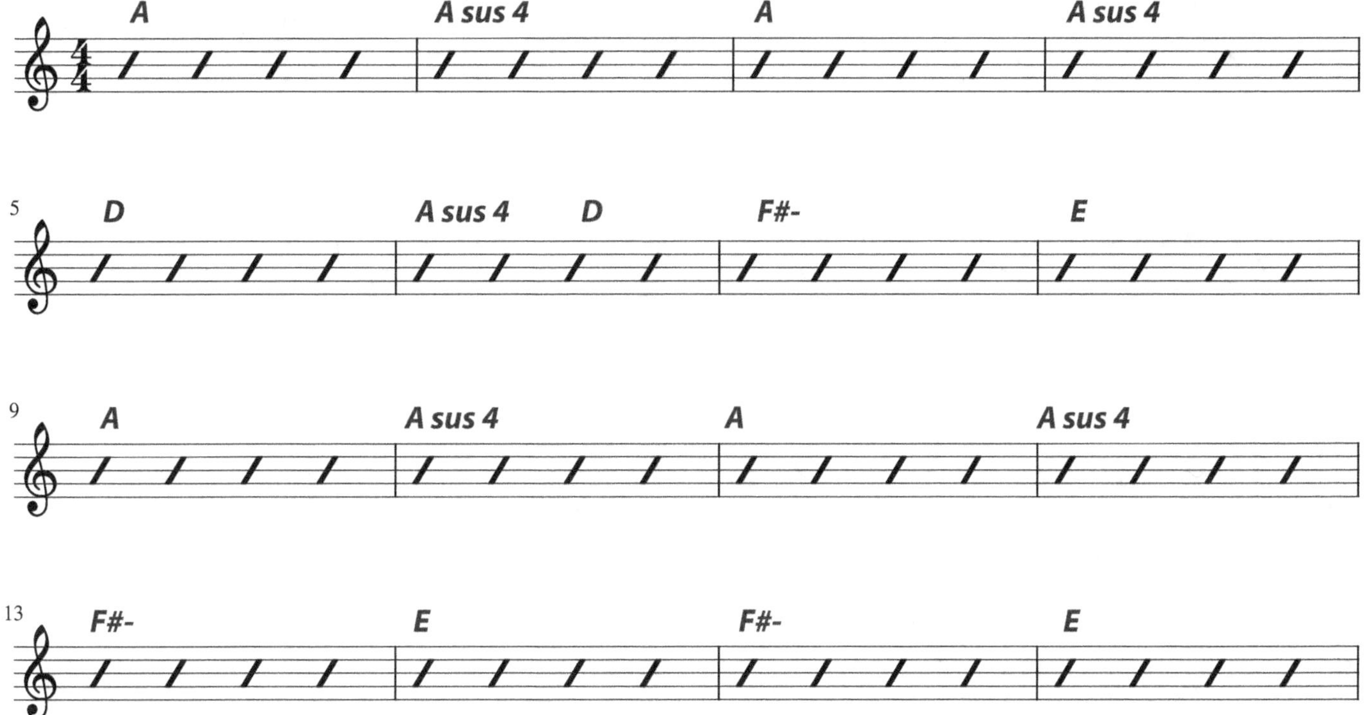

Sixteen Bars Verse

Many songs have a 16 bar structure for verse instead of eight bars. The example here is showing one way to create 16 bar verses by looking at it as two 8 bar versus with a variation of the last four bars. This simplifies writing 16 bar verse because you are only writing four different measures. It must be stressed that above all the melody of the song must go with the chords.

Chord, function in the last four measure shifts to the one and five repeated twice. Even though chord functions have changed in the structure with the last four measures the overall feel of the first 12 measures kept within the one and four context apart from the five chord in the last measure of the first eight bars.

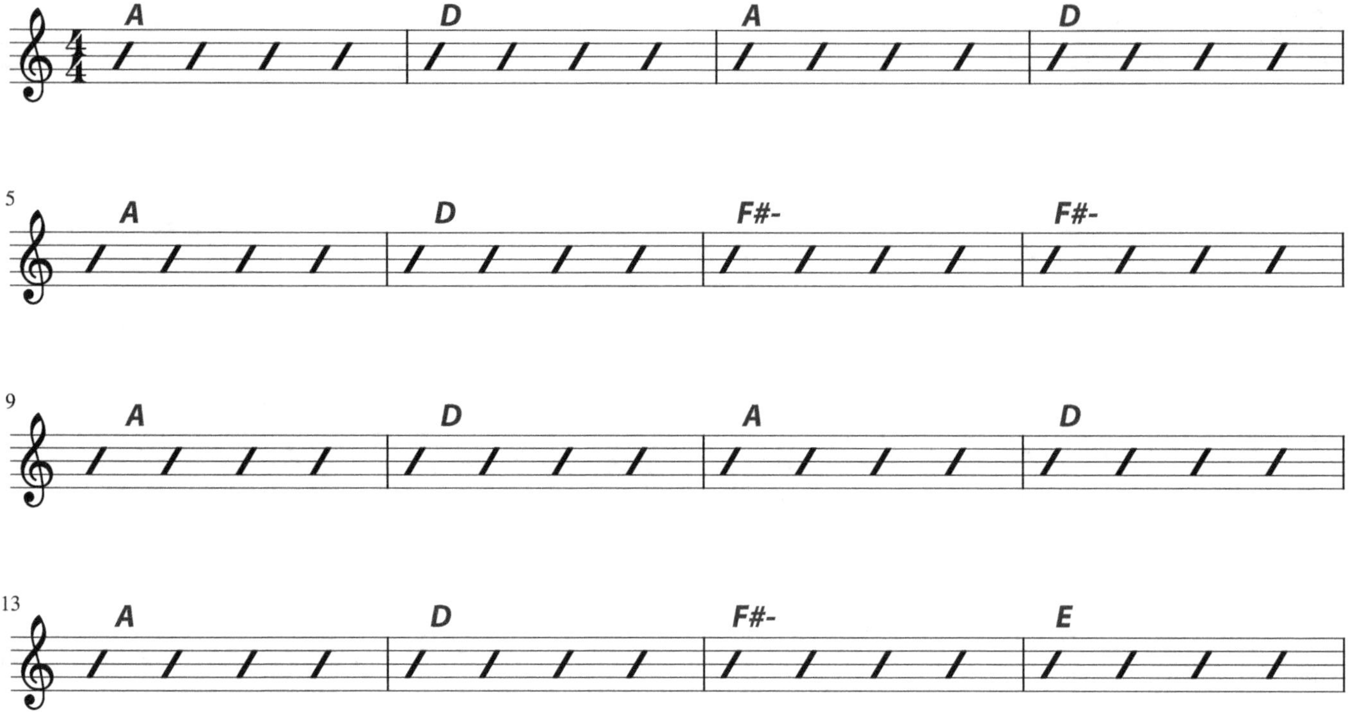

Expanding on the Sixteen Bar Verse

The F# minor chord in measures seven and eight can be thought of as either the one function, or the four. It is theoretically speaking the six chord in the key of A. However, just looking at it that way and not thinking of it is how it can function, as either the one or four chord, you never really see the purpose of going to F# minor. The thought process here is to use it as a means to stay within the one and four chord structure for the first eight bars.

As you can see the last measure goes to the five chord. This allows for a chorus or another verse to start a new Loop.

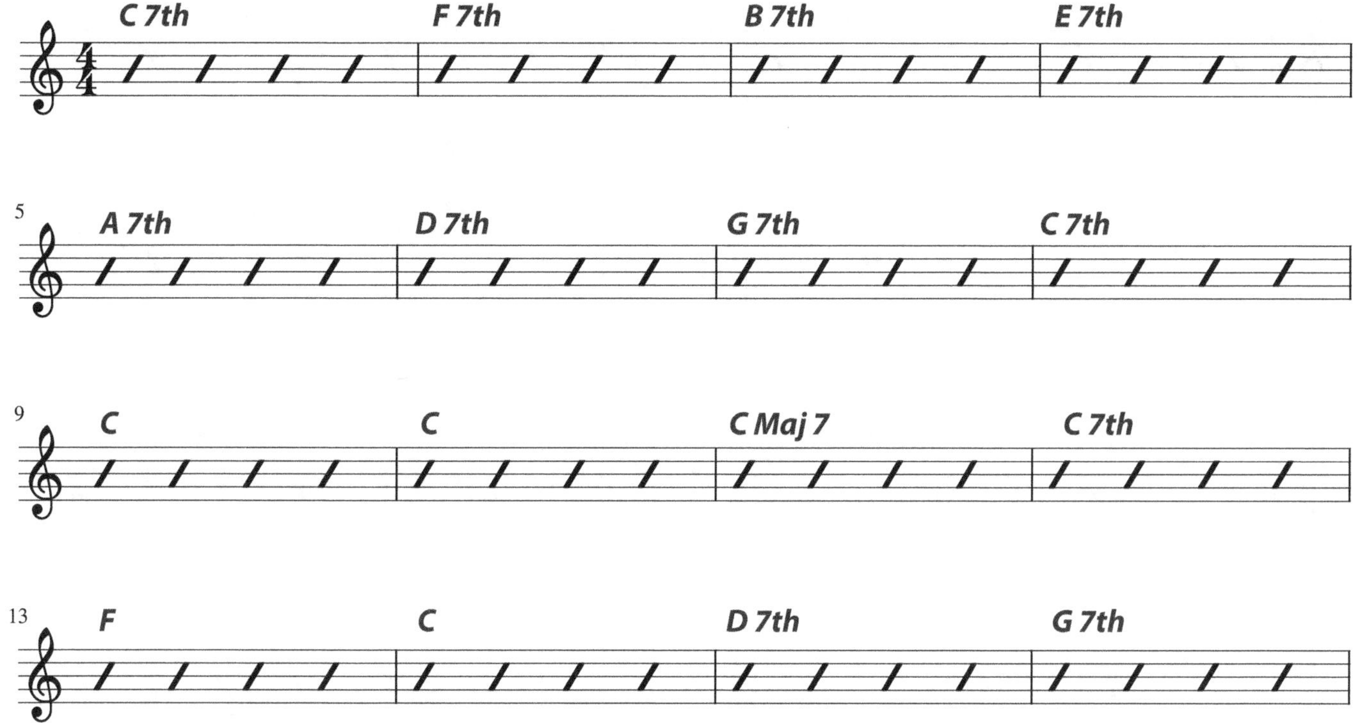

One	Two	Three	Four	Five	Six	Seven
C7	D7	E7	F7	G7	A7	B7
F Major	G Major	A Major	Bb Major	C Major	D Major	E Major
F minor	G minor	A minor	Bb minor	C minor	D minor	E minor

Using Secondary Dominants

The use of secondary dominants is a means to break up the predictability of what a key is going to sound like. The first set of staff lines has turned every chord in C, to a dominant seventh chord. Every key can be thought of as having seven secondary dominant chords.

The second set of eight bars gives you an example of how the D7 was used as a secondary dominant in an 8 bar progression. The table gives you a guide to how to use secondary dominant chords. The table illustrates how they can lead to major chords a 4th up or a minor chord a fourth up from the dominant chord you are Playing.

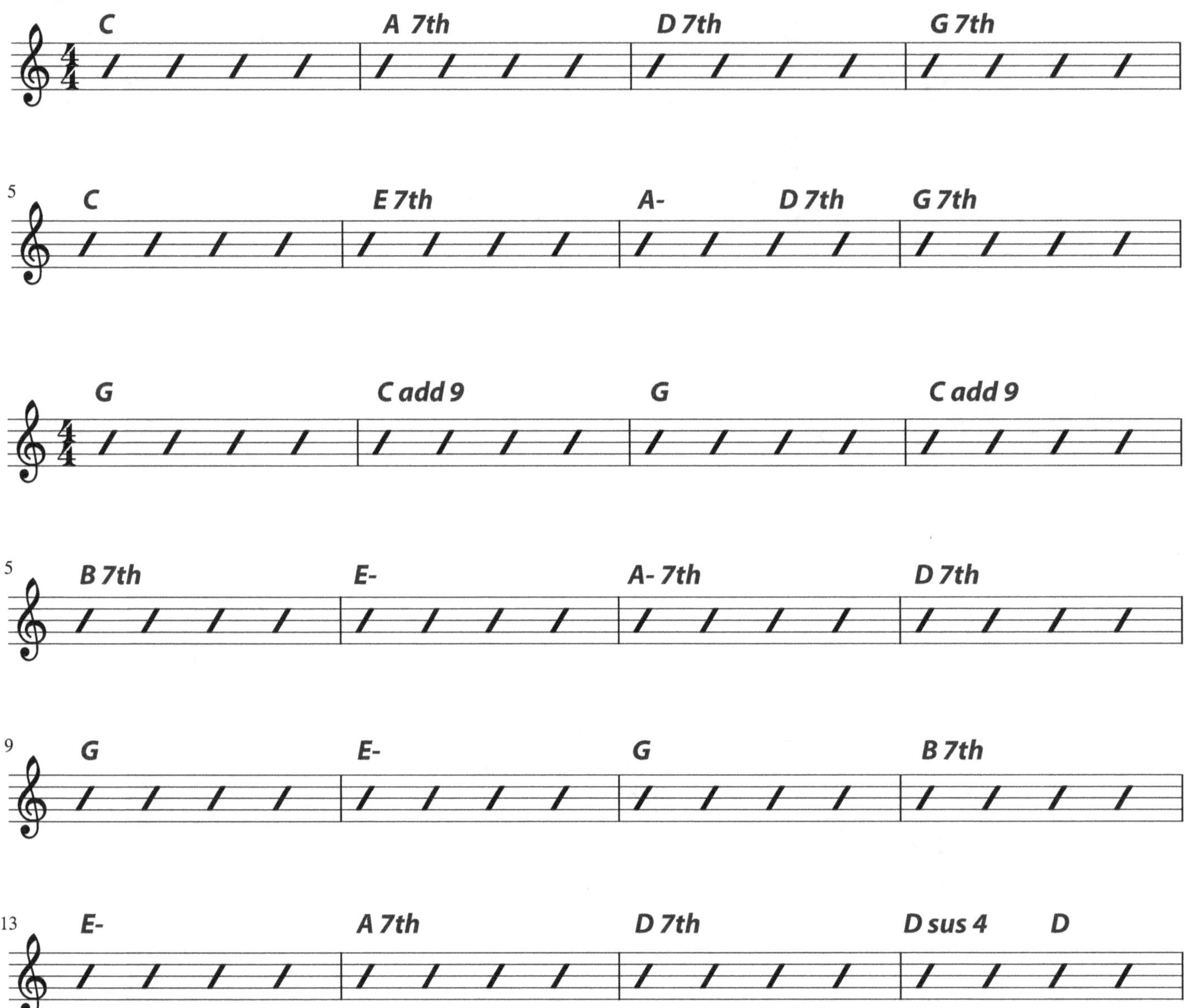

Secondary Dominants Applied to Eight Bar and Sixteen Bar Verses

Secondary dominants allow a progression to have chord movement this can take a song to a place that really makes it have something special rather than just staying in the same key. The use of several secondary dominant chords that move in four root notes from each other can be used to lead back to the one chord where the progression began.

If you study the chart on secondary dominants you will see how they all have been used in every example given. It is especially important to understand chord function and the number of each of the chords applied to each chord in a key as to what key the examples are in so you can use the theory with your own Writing.

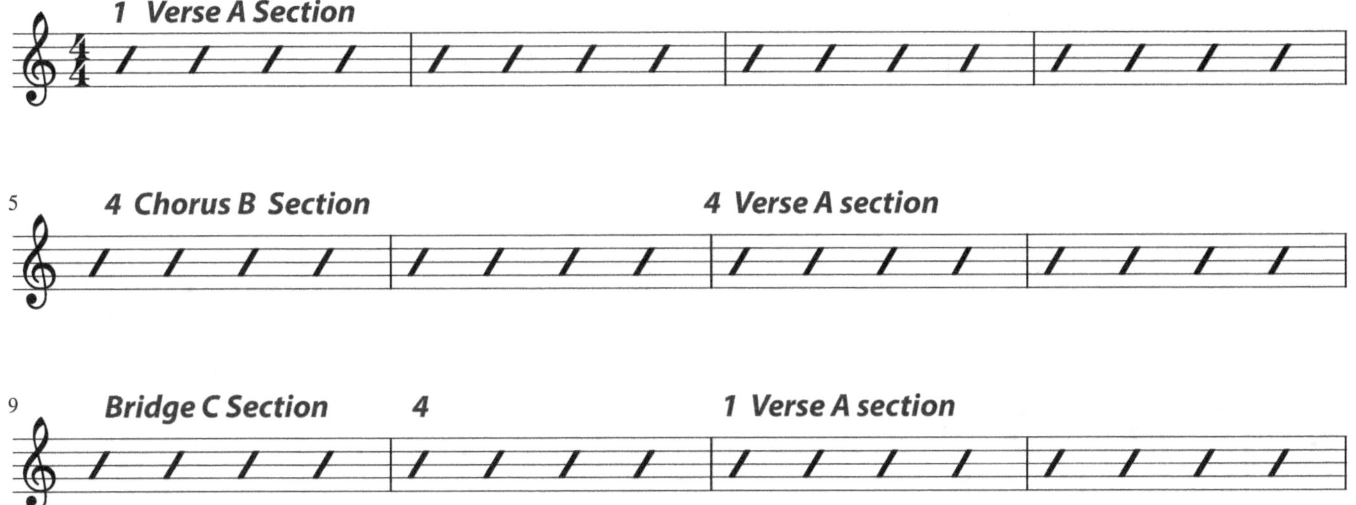

A B A C A Song Form

Our music today has its roots in the Blues. Before the Blues there was classical music (serious Music), which has a lot of influence in our pop music culture, but without the Blues there would be no jazz, rock, metal, country, fusion and progressive styles of music.

The12 bar Blues form will be used to illustrate song form in many ways and you will begin to see how this form guided pop artists in their writing. The Blues influenced all pop artists intentionally and some indirectly, but without the Blues they would not be what they are today.

Jazz is a musical child of the Blues. First there was Blues then ragtime and then jazz forms developed. The Blues is a foundation of so much of our phrasing vocally as well as solos on instruments. Once the Blues was introduced into our musical world it became the springboard to deviate from a lot of diatonic harmony (one key).

The 12 bar form at the top has verse for the one chord, Chorus for the four chord, and bridge for the five chord, creating the A B A C A Song form. Artists either knowingly or not, learned song form from the Blues as the means to create verse chorus and bridge sections of a song.

In the lessons so far you have been given examples that combine the A and B sections of the Blues, using the one and four chords, to create the A section in mostly the same key. The purpose of that was to illustrate how eight bars with the A section could be developed and then that was extended to sixteen bars for the A sections.

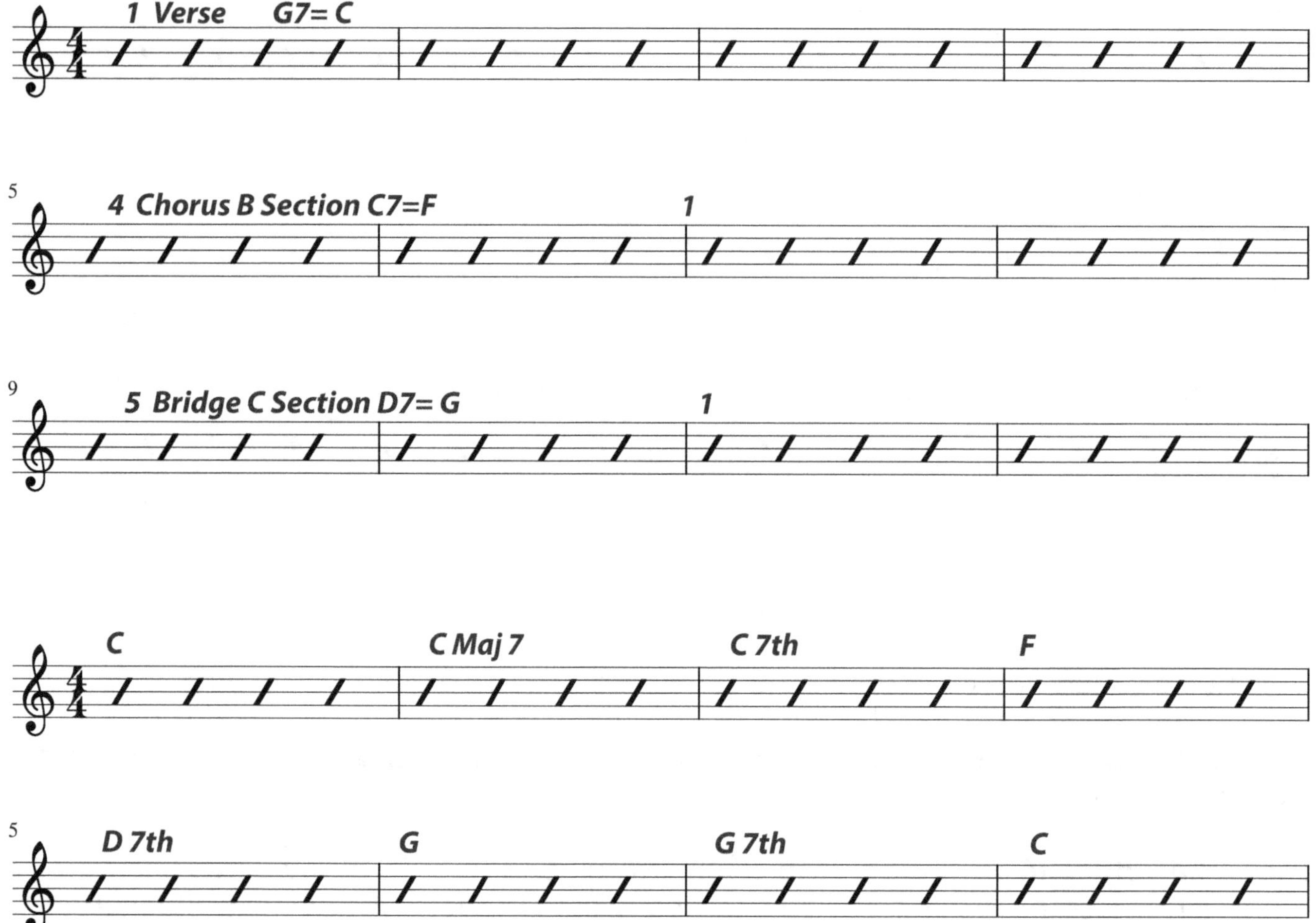

Understanding the Blues Harmonically

The Blues can be thought of as a form of music in three different key centers when you apply traditional music theory to it. The seventh chords can be thought of as the five chords of each key. When you do this, you begin to see the blueprint or musical D N A For the evolution of our pop music culture. Artist either knew the dominant chords functioned as secondary dominants and how they resolved or just heard it. Either way, they used the examples of secondary dominant chords in their compositions.

Understanding the three keys can open a world of creativity as you will see.

The eight bar example above could easily be used as a section of a song you are writing as it has been used by many songwriters.

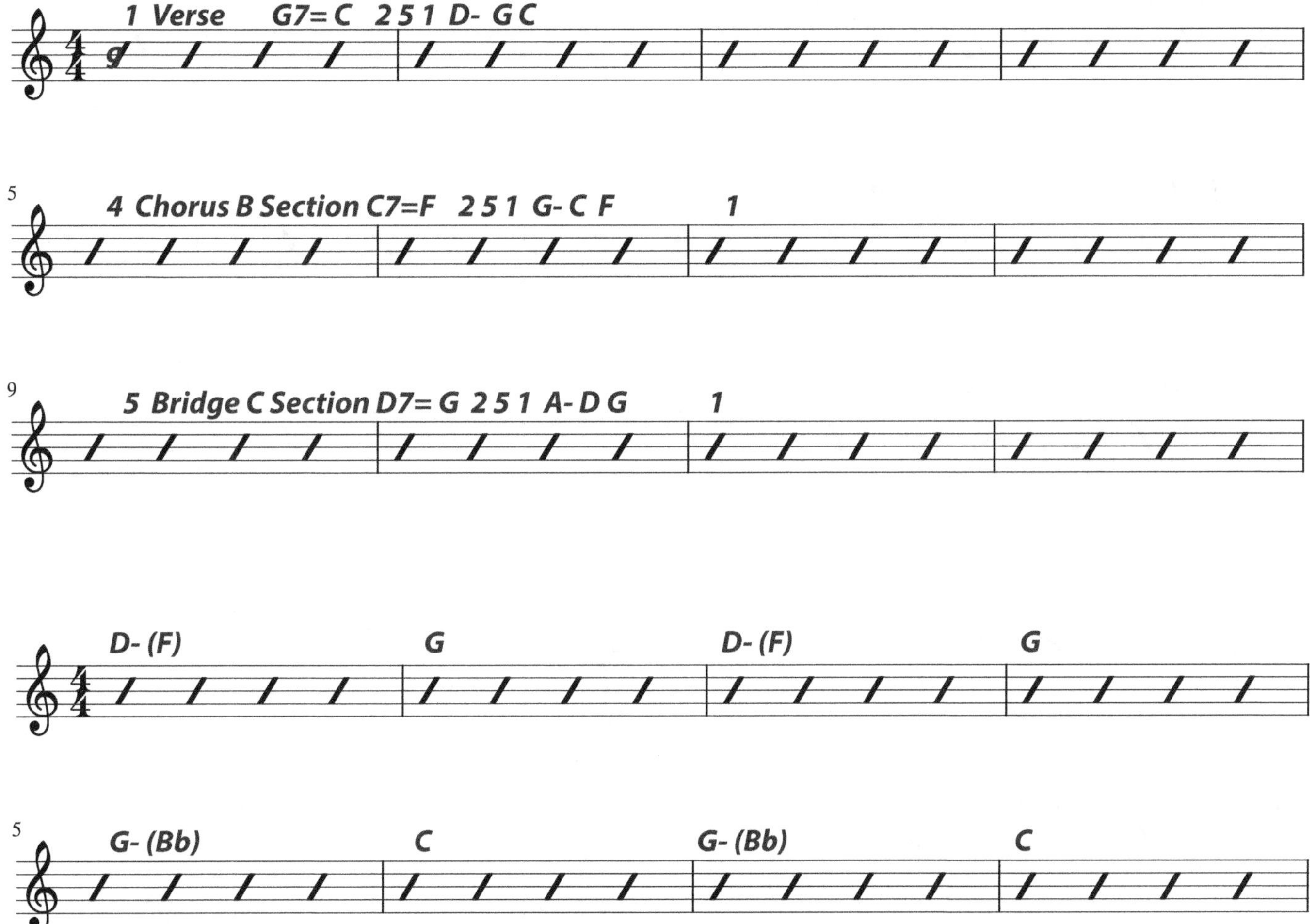

Using the Two- Five- One Chord Progression

The two-five- one sequence is found all over jazz, and because it was done before rock or other forms of pop music we have today, it has been used by many pop songwriters as a means to write chord progressions. In the example above you see the two keys of C and F, with the two and five chords for both keys.

The D minor chord is related to F and the G minor chord is related to B flat. This was discussed in previous lessons; the one major chord can be used in place of the six minor chord. Therefore, they both are presented as options, or substitutions.

The major chords give the progression a more rock or pop feel. The minor chords are more subtle in feel.

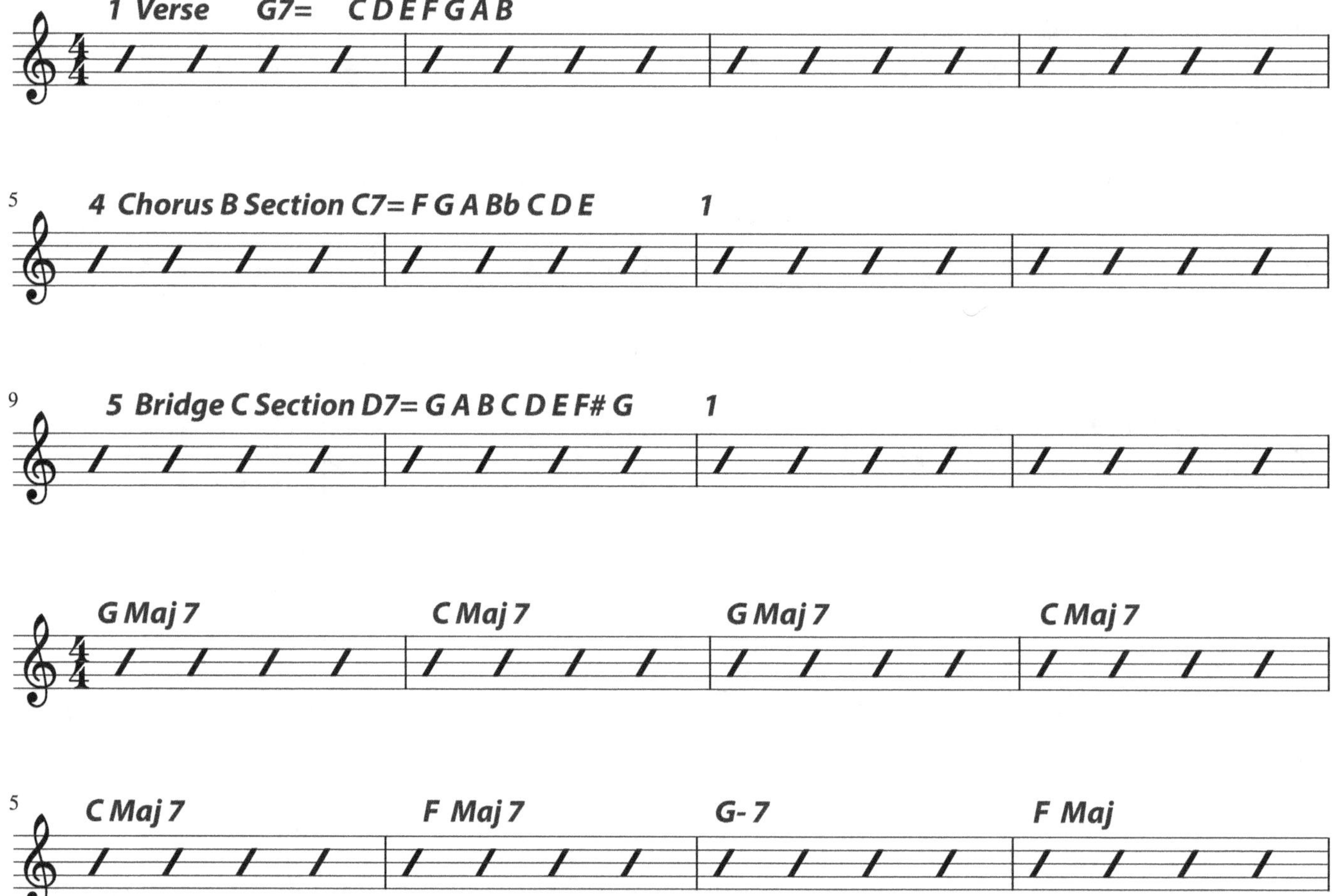

Close Key Modulations

The Blues in its three-chord structure was considerably basic and never destined to dominate the music world with constant number one hits. The artist who grew up playing the Blues and becoming world famous knew this, and that is why they ventured away from the standard three chord form. But what they learned was how this structure could be used to write so much more music because of the three keys and their relationship with each other. They either developed this by trial and error or studied it.

This relationship of three keys found in the Blues is laced throughout classical music and it's called close key modulations. It also is a large part of the circle of fifths, which will be discussed soon. The example in this lesson can be found in many songs in the 60s and 70s. The use of major seven chords as illustrated here are from the keys of G, C, and F

Key to the left	Center key	Key to the right
F G A Bb C D E F	C D E F G A B C	G A B C D E F# G
C D E F G A B D	G A B C D E F# G	D E F# G A B C# D
G A B C D E F# G	D E F# G A B C# D	A B C# D E F# G# A
D E F# G A B C# D	A B C# D E F# G# A	E F# G# A B C# D# E
A B C# D E F# G# A	E F# G# A B C# D# E	B C# D# E F# G# A# B
E F# G# A B C# D# E	B C# D# E F# G# A# B	F# G# A# B C# D# E# F#
B C# D# E F# G# A# B	F# G# A# B C# D# E# F#	Db Eb F Gb Ab Bb C Db
Gb Ab Bb C Db Eb F G Ab	Db Eb F Gb Ab Bb C Db	Ab Bb C Db Eb F G Ab
Db Eb F Gb Ab Bb C Db	Ab Bb C Db Eb F G Ab	Eb F G Ab Bb C D Eb
Ab Bb C Db Eb F G Ab	Eb F G Ab Bb C D Eb	Bb C D Eb F G A Bb
Eb F G Ab Bb C D Eb	Bb C D Eb F G A Bb	F G A Bb C D E F
Bb C D Eb F G A Bb	F G A Bb C D E F	C D E F G A B C
Key to the left	**Center key**	**Key to the right**

Close Key Modulations

Sitting down to write music is not as hard when you have several tools at your disposal to do so. The best songs come through inspiration, and no one can argue that fact. When times of inspiration are not generous to us, we can rely on knowledge, and that can spark creativity. Knowledge can lead us to a path, we may not have been going down in a song. One of the most important things you can know as a songwriter, is the keys that are close to the one you are writing in for a main melody. For example if the main melody theme is in the key of C the other two keys close to C are F and G.

This can be put into a formula to remember by thinking of the key of F as a fifth down from C, (D E F G). You can also get a visual image if you imagine C as the key in the center of F to the left, and G to the right. Study the table above that has all the keys. The center key, left and key to the right notice the difference in the notes is only one note for the center key when you go to the left or right.

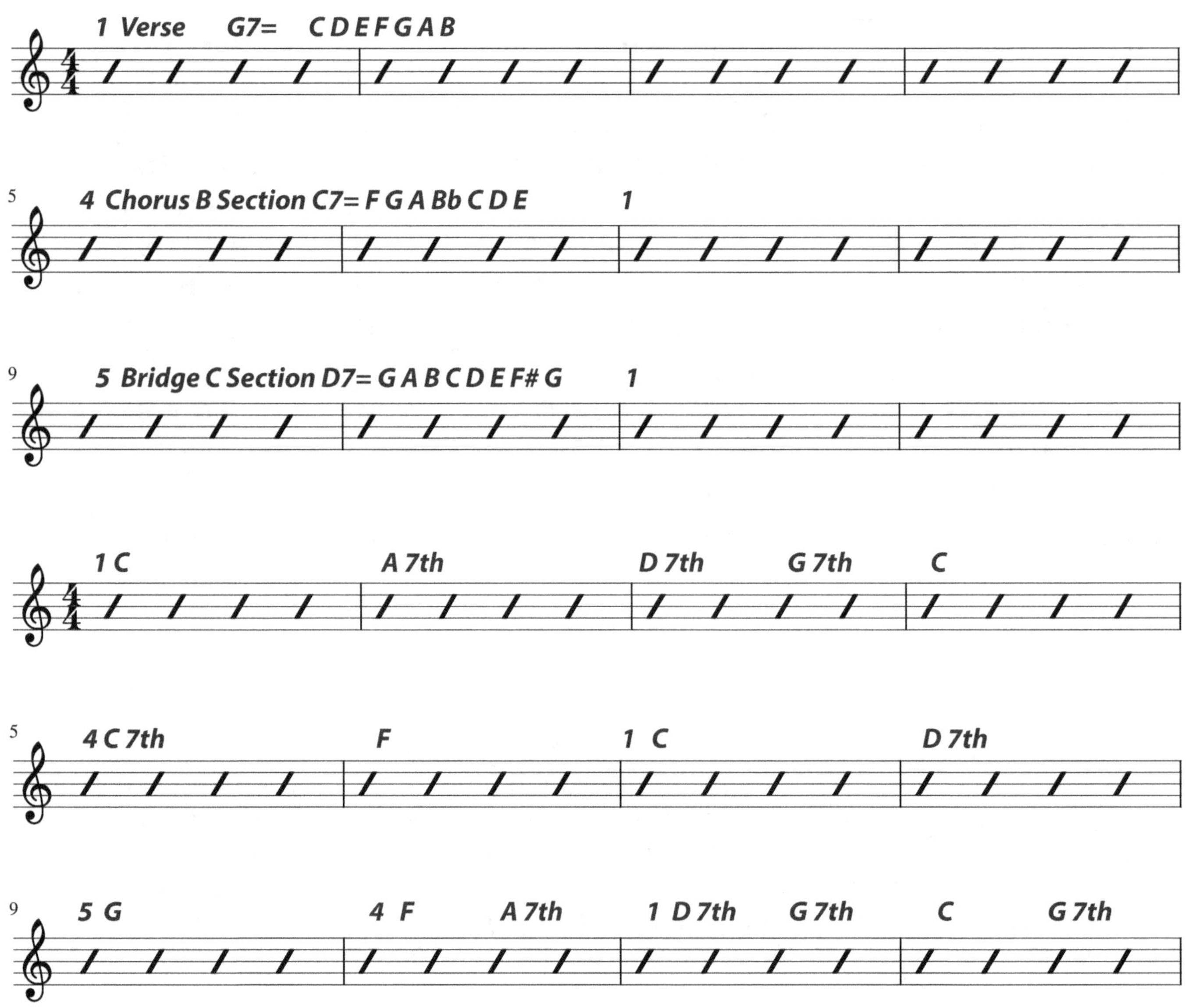

Close Key Modulations

The 6-2-5-1 sequence is based on root notes that are a fourth apart from one another. In the key of C, the root notes would be (A D G C). However, the kind of chords Used for root notes, referred to as quality of chords, meaning major, minor, or dominant does not have to be in the key. The purpose of the root notes moving in this fashion, is to create chord movement and this keeps the chords from being stagnant.

There is the implied harmony of the three keys at various places in this example, with the one chord, starting in measures one and four. The four chord in the six measure preceded by the C7 chord. The one chord was used in the 7th measure followed by D7 to lead to the five chord G, in the ninth major. The 10th measure started with F and then the sequence is 6-2-5-1 used to get back to C.

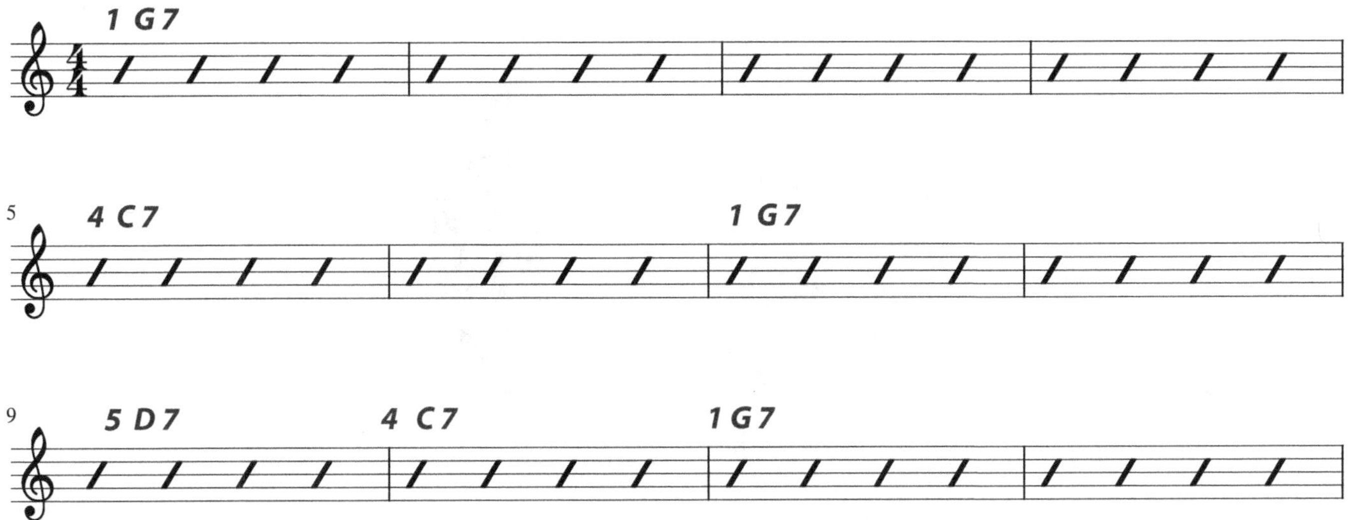

Hidden Treasures in the Blues

When you look at the 12 bar Blues above do you see more than just three chords? If your answer is yes then you had your eyes opened to a lot of what many famous artists today did. They journeyed through this progression and evolved and became the songwriters they are with this foundation.

The first thing to realize is the framework of three parts. The three parts could be the A section (verse), B section (chorus), and C section (bridge) of a song. So, songs that were written by artists who started out playing the Blues learned song form from the Blues.

Artists from The Beatles, Rolling Stones, and all those that followed them in the British invasion, learn from the Blues in how to write songs with this form. Section 4 used the 12 bar Blues to illustrate song form jazz artists, country artists and pop artists used and were directly or indirectly influenced from this three chord progression.

Putting chord progressions or loops together can be seen from the Blues if you understand keys, and chord function with in those keys. Section 4 taught you a lot about chord functions and showed you all seven chords can function as the one, four, and five chords.

The use of secondary dominants was introduced and shown how to use them in song form. With the secondary dominants you were shown how to resolve them so they can be used in your songwriting.

Section 4 introduced you to close key modulations and used the Blues to illustrate that it is a form that is based around close key modulations. This will help you out tremendously as was illustrated with several examples.

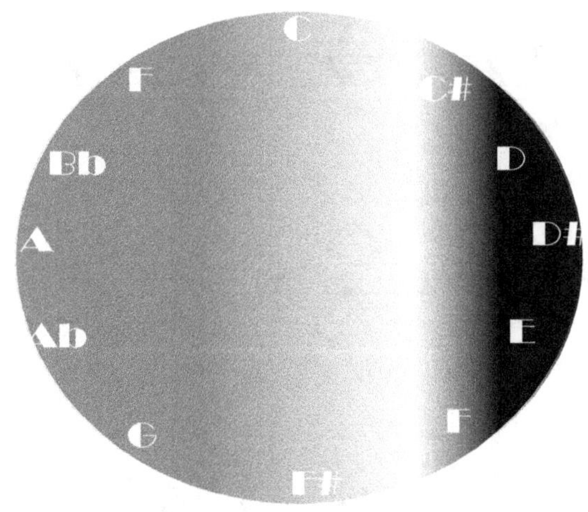

F G A Bb C D E F	C D E F G A B C	G A B C D E F# G
C D E F G A B D	G A B C D E F# G	D E F# G A B C# D
G A B C D E F# G	D E F# G A B C# D	A B C# D E F# G# A
D E F# G A B C# D	A B C# D E F# G# A	E F# G# A B C# D# E
A B C# D E F# G# A	E F# G# A B C# D# E	B C# D# E F# G# A# B
E F# G# A B C# D# E	B C# D# E F# G# A# B	F# G# A# B C# D# E# F#
B C# D# E F# G# A# B	F# G# A# B C# D# E# F#	Db Eb F Gb Ab Bb C Db
Gb Ab Bb C Db Eb F G Ab	Db Eb F Gb Ab Bb C Db	Ab Bb C Db Eb F G Ab
Db Eb F Gb Ab Bb C Db	Ab Bb C Db Eb F G Ab	Eb F G Ab Bb C D Eb
Ab Bb C Db Eb F G Ab	Eb F G Ab Bb C D Eb	Bb C D Eb F G A Bb
Eb F G Ab Bb C D Eb	Bb C D Eb F G A Bb	F G A Bb C D E F
Bb C D Eb F G A Bb	F G A Bb C D E F	C D E F G A B C
Key to the left	**Center key**	**Key to the right**

The Circle of Fifths

The Circle of fifths is one of the most important music devices for playing any instrument, writing songs, and something every serious songwriter should know! all 12 keys are taught using the circle of fifths, because each new key that is added from the previous key is only different by one note. Compare the key of C with the key of G, then G with the key of D and so on. You will see an order that helps you learn keys faster. If you compare the chords from the key of C with the chords from the key of G, you see four chords are the same in both keys.

The circle of fifths is a great way to practice everything you know, and will learn, because of a lot of songs used the circle of fifths for the way the melodies and chords were composed. As you practice with the circle of this you are building this way of thinking and hearing into your mind

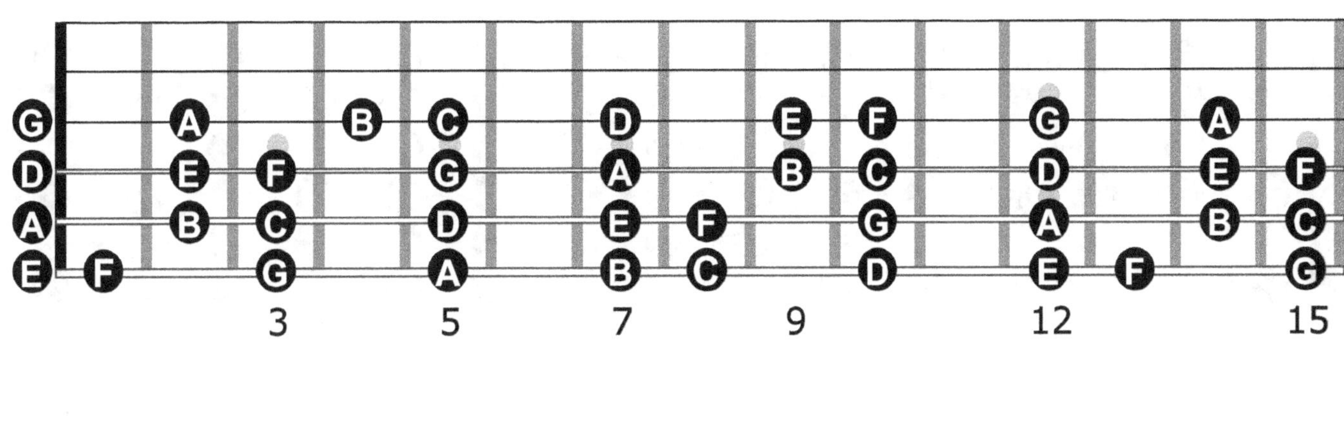

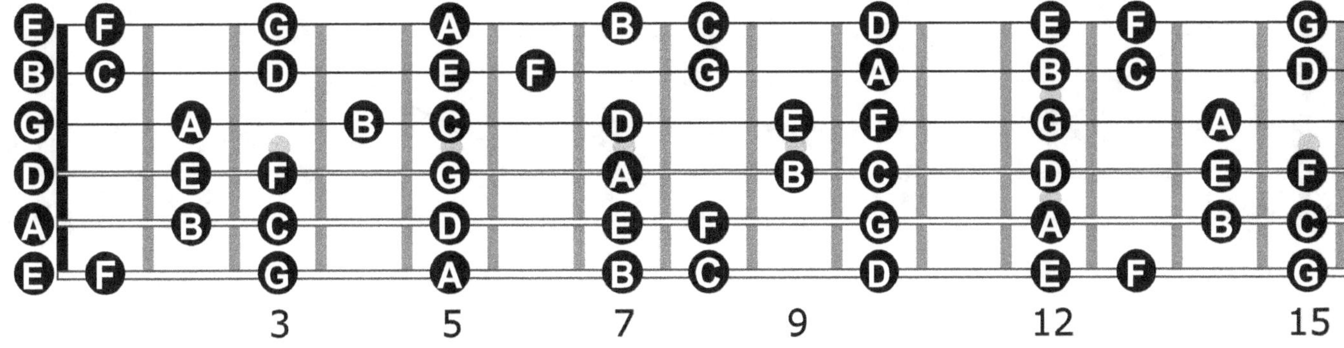

The Guitar starting on the third string and 4th string as a string pair all up the fret board has a pattern of five notes apart from one another, on each fret. Going in the opposite direction, from the 4th string to the third string the pattern is four notes. From the six string to the third string on each fret you can see the patterns all up and down the fret board are in fourths.

When it comes to the third and second string the 5th and fourth note pattern is broken. From the third string to the second string the pattern is thirds. The pattern of fourths resumes from the 2nd and 1st strings.

The pattern of fourths from the six string to the third string is going around the circle counterclockwise. Going from the third string to the six string in fifths , is clockwise. learning to use the fretboard with the circle of fifths for chords and scales is not difficult when you understand the structure of how notes are organized up and down the fret board from string to string. Study the fret board diagrams, And practice saying the notes on each fret that has been illustrated for the key of C.

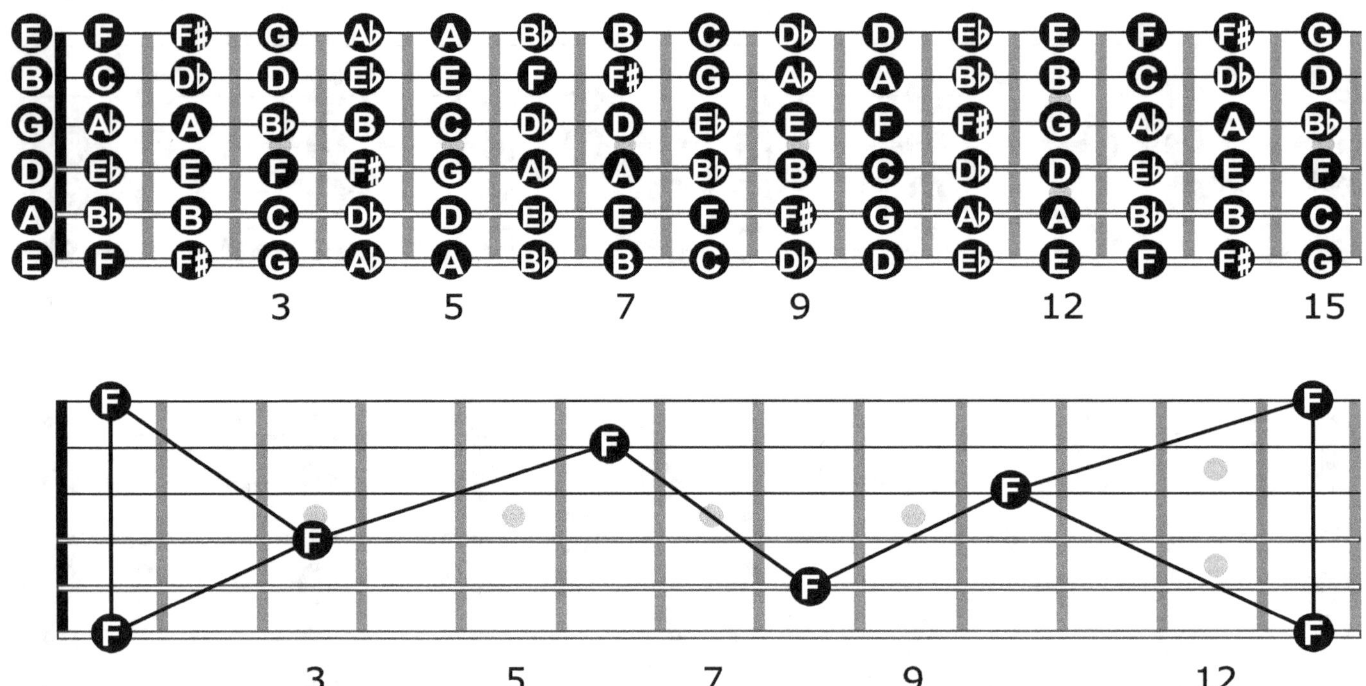

Notes and Octave Centers

The notes on the first diagram illustrate the five different octave centers that start on the first fret. All notes on the guitar can be seen with these five octave centers. Octave center 1 has 3 F notes memorized, the pattern. Notice the six string, 4th string, have a three- fret span. The F on the first string is easy because the six string and 1st strings are the same notes on every fret.

The F on the 4th string an F on the second string have a four- fret span. The third octave center is from the fifth string F to the second-string half, this octave center has two adjacent strings that separate them. It also spans 3 frets like the first octave center does.

Octave center 4, is from the fifth string to the third string, and it has a 3- fret span. The last octave center has 3 F notes, and it span's four frets.
These octave centers are a tremendous way to learn all the notes on the fret board.

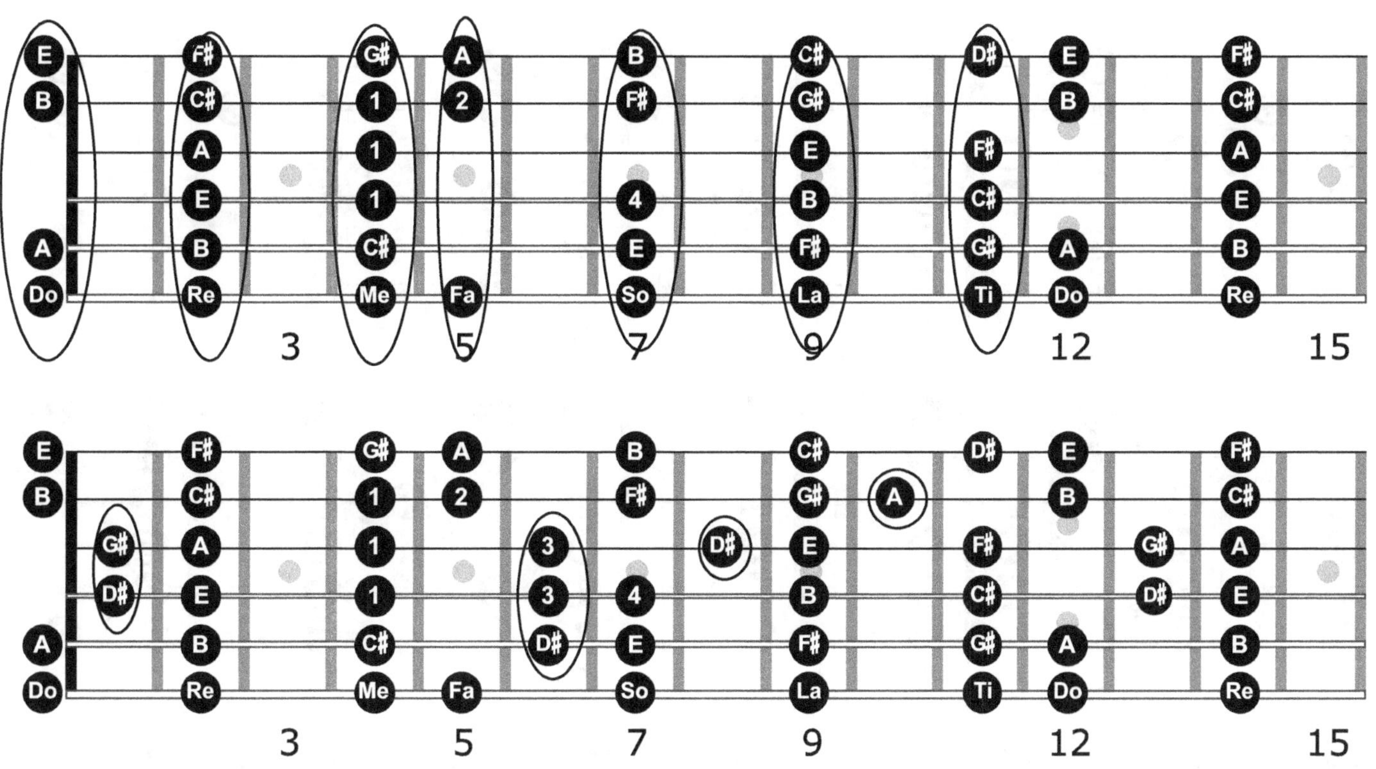

Do	RE	Me	Fa	So	La	Ti
4	6	6	3	5	6	5

Visualizing Every Key

The table and diagrams are illustrating a way to see every key with seven vertical fret patterns, and the notes on all the strings for each fret pattern. The first diagram has the seven fret patterns, and the second diagram has the notes in between each vertical pattern highlighted with ovals.

The table illustrates where you find Do on the six string for each key, and illustrates there will be 4 notes, they are on the 6th, 5th, 2nd and 1st strings. Where Re, is there are six notes and so on with each of the vertical fret patterns. Learning to see the fret patterns, will help you visualize every key.

In between fret patterns you have notes and they are illustrated on the second diagram.

When you see a full fretboard diagram try to visualize the fret patterns illustrated here.

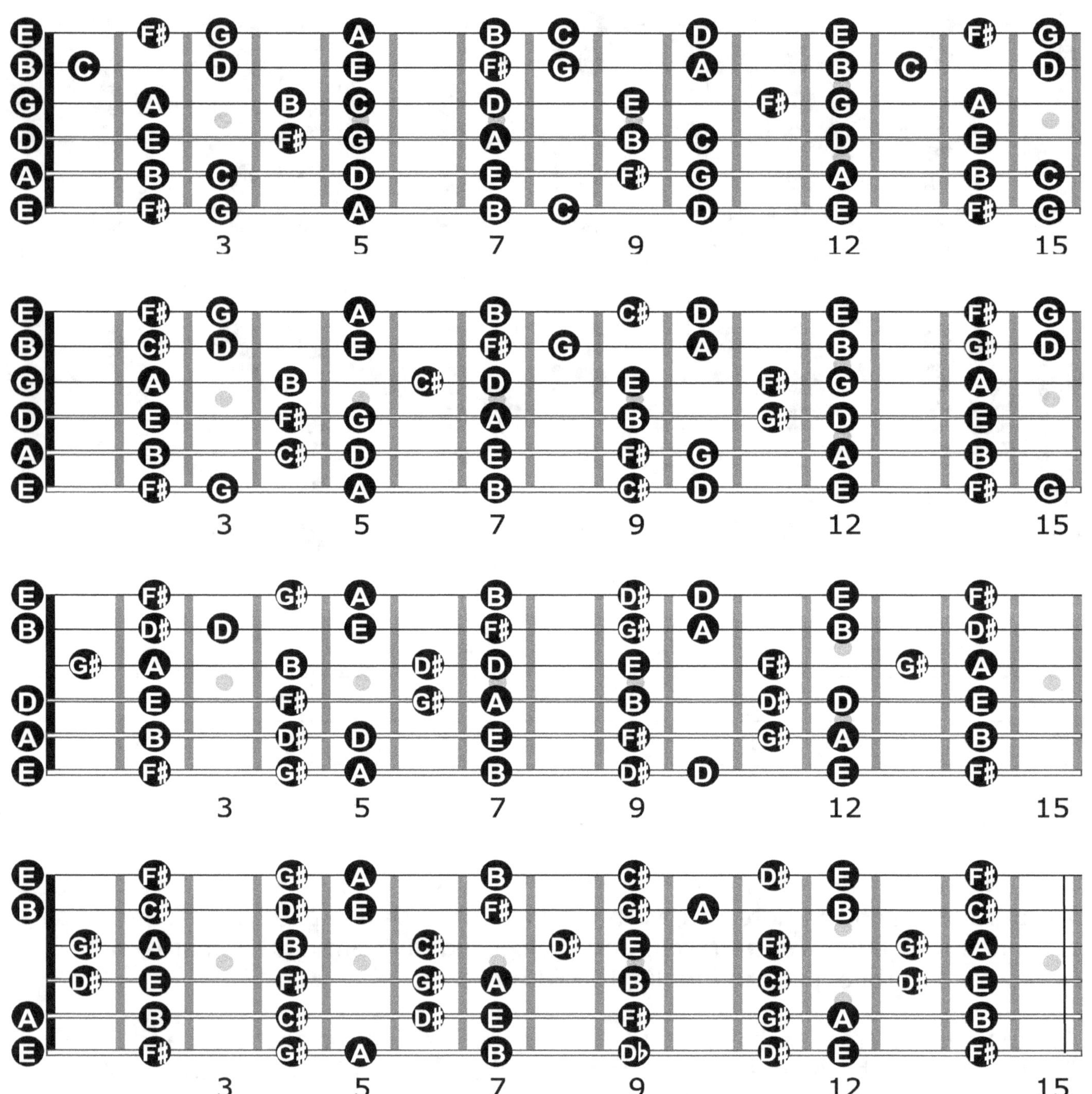

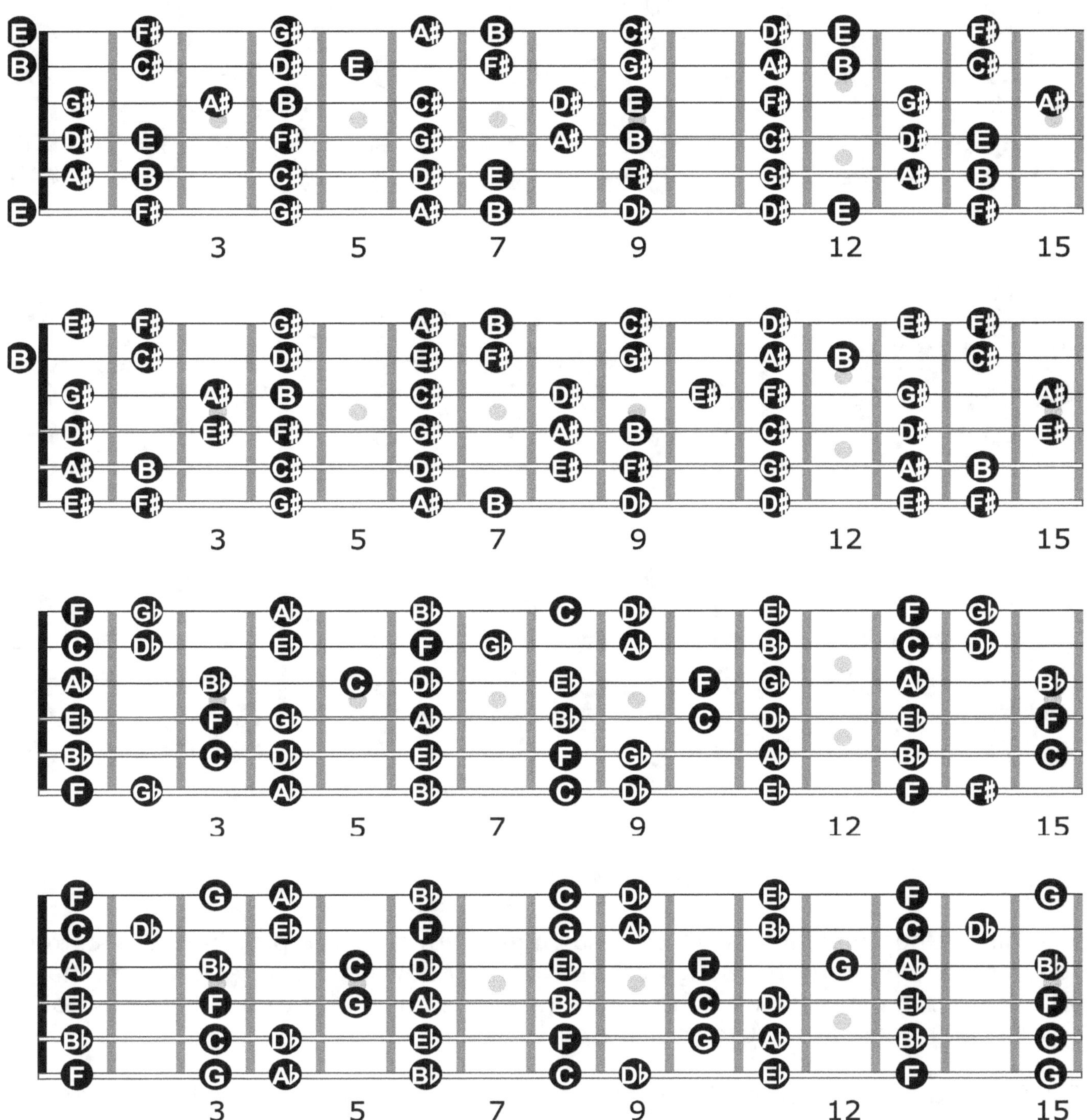

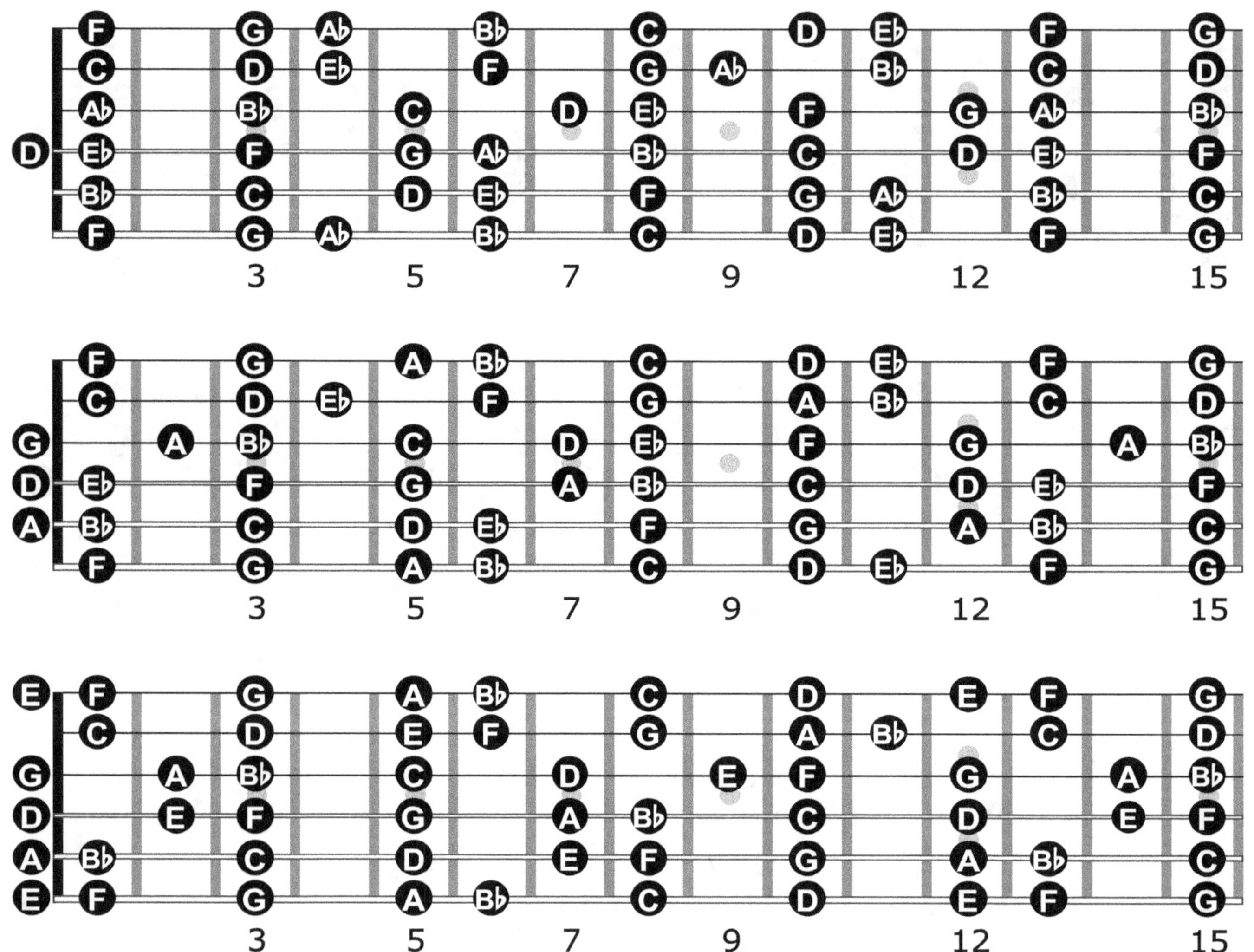

Notes in All 12 Keys

The full fret board diagrams will serve as a guide to help you play in whatever key you need to play in for the songs you're writing. Knowing the notes that you may be singing in a melody for a song you're writing is important to understand what chords you're going to put to your melody.

The full fretboard patterns with all the notes Should be looked at with the vertical fret patterns that have been presented as a means to help you visualize the notes in all the keys. The lessons as you continue in this study will now require you to understand the circle of fifths, and the notes in all 12 keys.

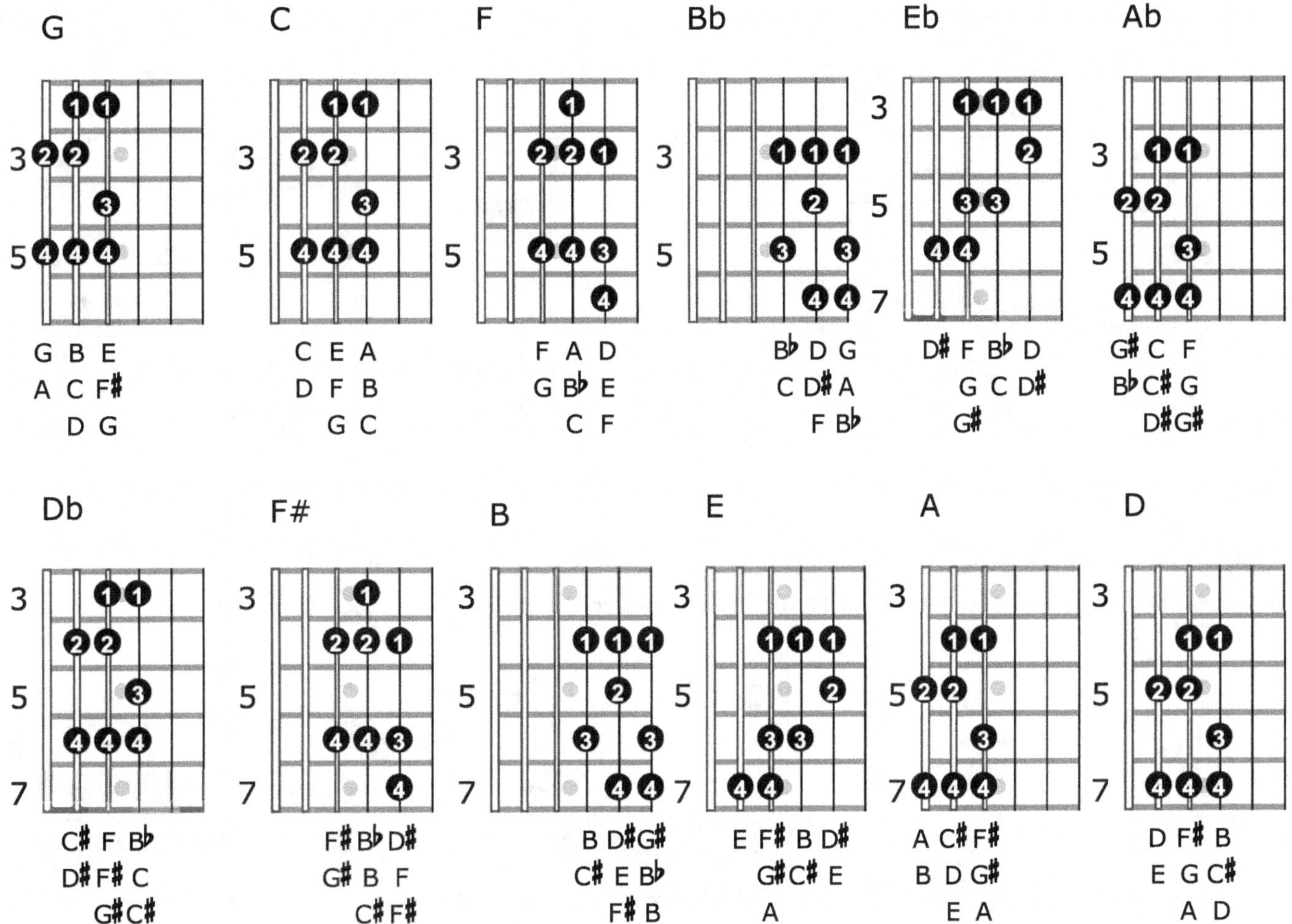

Scale Patterns Around the Circle

All scales and chords can be played around the circle of fifths this way these patterns illustrate how to use the way the guitar is tuned to play every key using the circle of fifths or going the opposite direction a circular fourths, As you see here going from G to see and so forth.

The cycle can start all over on C on the six string and start around the circle again. You can start on any note and go around the circle till you are back where you started.

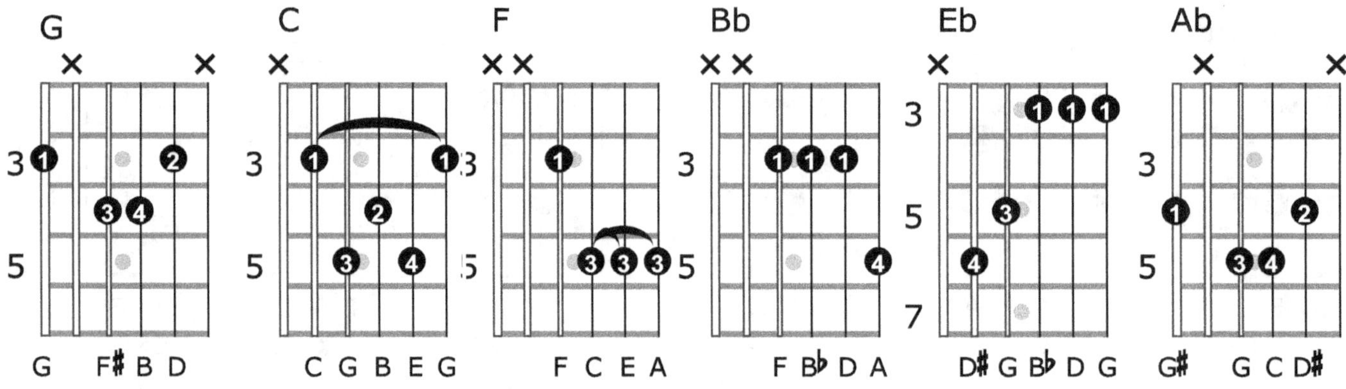

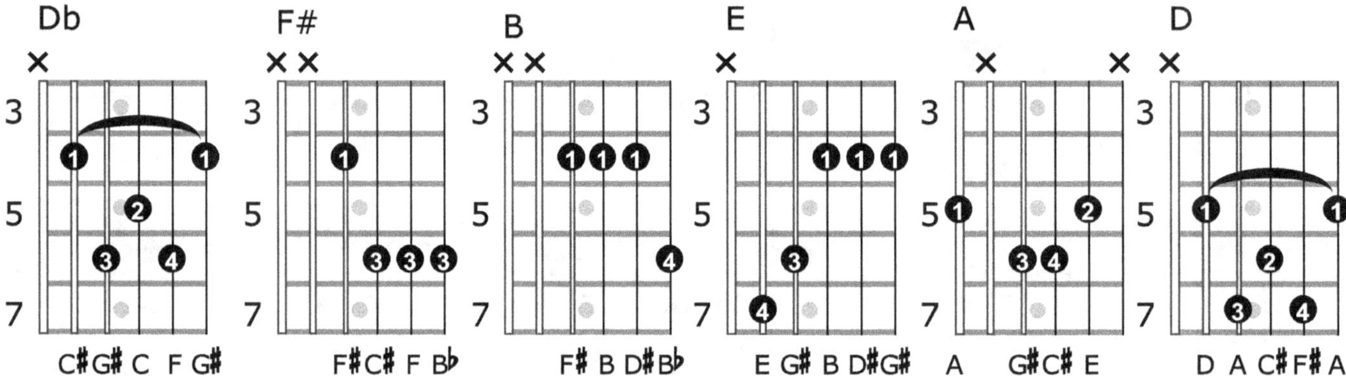

Major Seventh Chords Around the Circle

These chords above are major 7 chords and they can all become minor chords and 7th chords by altering the 3rd and 7th notes as has been explained in previous lessons.

The purpose of all the lessons you have had that illustrate circle movement is here to guide you in learning to use the tuning of your guitar with circle movement. This is a great way to learn keys with chords and scales.

Circle of Fifths

The circle of fifths is the best way to learn the guitar and understand it and make the most of your ability to learn the guitar. This section provides new ways of learning the notes on the fretboard. It helps you to learn chords and scales. The knowledge of the circle of the fifths, requires a lot of academics but its worth it to understand how it can benefit your song writing. Close key modulations are a part of the circle of fifths, and the knowledge of it and the use of it helped many song writers compose.

Close key Modulations

Close key modulations are a part of the circle of fifths, and the knowledge of it and the use of it helped many song writers compose. The great composers like Bach, Mozart, and so many used the circle of fifths, and close keys separated by one note different from each other. This is a great way to change keys. A table was given that illustrated how to learn close keys and use them with a center key and the two other
Keys close to it.

Tips for Practicing

Section five covered great tips for practicing chord, and scales, and understand the way the guitar is tuned in standard tuning. The knowledge of the circle of fifths was applied to aid in learning

to practice chords and scales. Every major key was given in full fretboard form around the circle. Chords and scale patterns were illustrated on the fretboard with the circle of fifths to help you apply root movement for chords and scales using the sixth and fifth strings.

Ionian	M 2	M 2	m 2	M 2	M 2	M 2	m 2
Dorian	M 2	m 2	M 2	M 2	M 2	m 2	M 2
Phrygian	m 2	M 2	M 2	M 2	m 2	M 2	M 2
Lydian	M 2	M 2	M 2	m 2	M 2	M 2	m 2
Mixolydian	M 2	M 2	m 2	M 2	M 2	m 2	M 2
Aeolian	M 2	m 2	M 2	M 2	m 2	M 2	M 2
Locrian	m 2	M 2	M 2	m 2	M 2	M 2	M 2

C- Ionian	D	E	F	G	A	B	C
D- Dorian	E	F	G	A	B	C	D
E- Phrygian	F	G	A	B	C	D	E
F- Lydian	G	A	B	C	D	E	F
G- Mixolydian	A	B	C	D	E	F	G
A-Aeolian	B	C	D	E	F	G	A
B-Locrian	C	D	E	F	G	A	B

Modes of the Major Scale.

Learning to use the modes is where your writing will take on more depth with melodic and harmonic definition. The first table above has how each mode is constructed, with major and minor seconds. The second table has all the modes from the key of C major. Practice Singing each mode to get the sounds of them in your ears.

The Ionian mode is just another name for the major scale. Each mode starts and ends on the other scale degrees of the major scale. Within the major scale there are six more modes besides the Ionian which is the major scale.

The seven modes can be studied as far as the origins with outside resources and research. The knowledge of their origins is not essential to know in order to use them. The structure of intervals of major and minor seconds is.

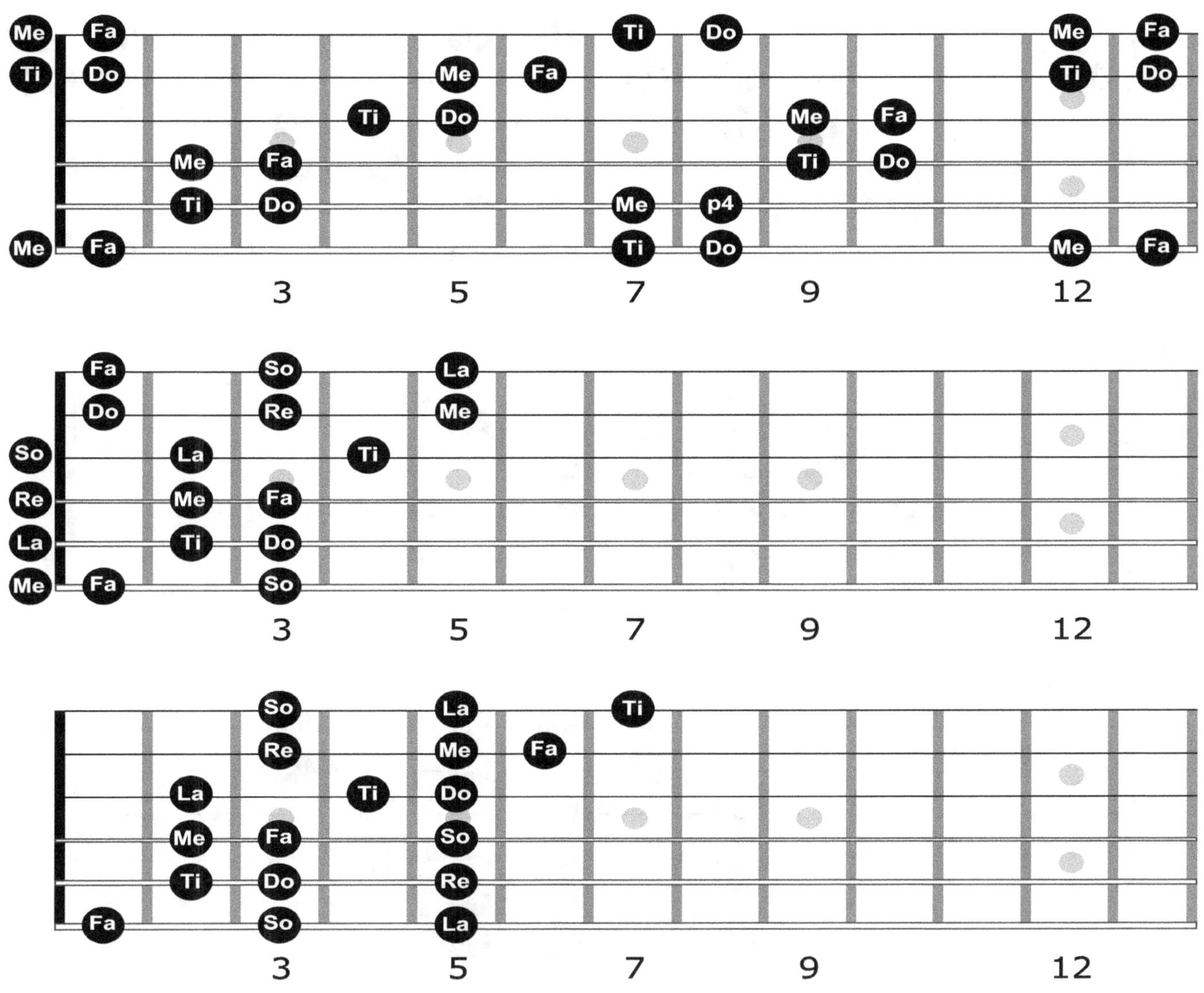

Ionian	Do	Re	Me	Fa	So	La	Ti	Do
Dorian	Re	Me	Fa	So	La	Ti	Do	Re
Phrygian	Me	Fa	So	La	Ti	Do	Re	Me
Lydian	Fa	So	La	Ti	Do	Re	Me	Fa
Mixolydian	So	La	Ti	Do	Re	Me	Fa	So
Aeolian	La	Ti	Do	Re	Me	Fa	So	La
Locrian	Ti	Do	Re	Me	Fa	So	La	Ti

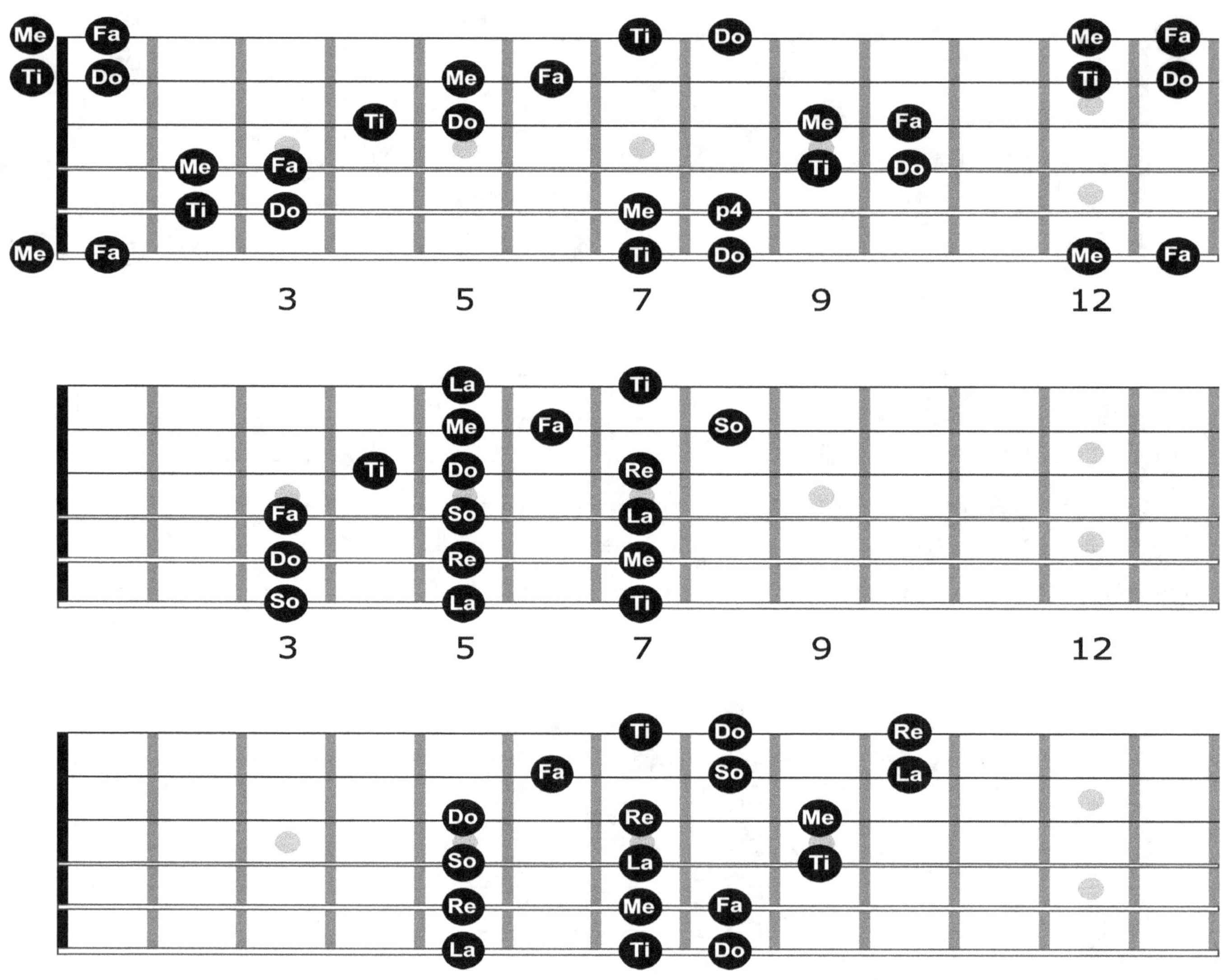

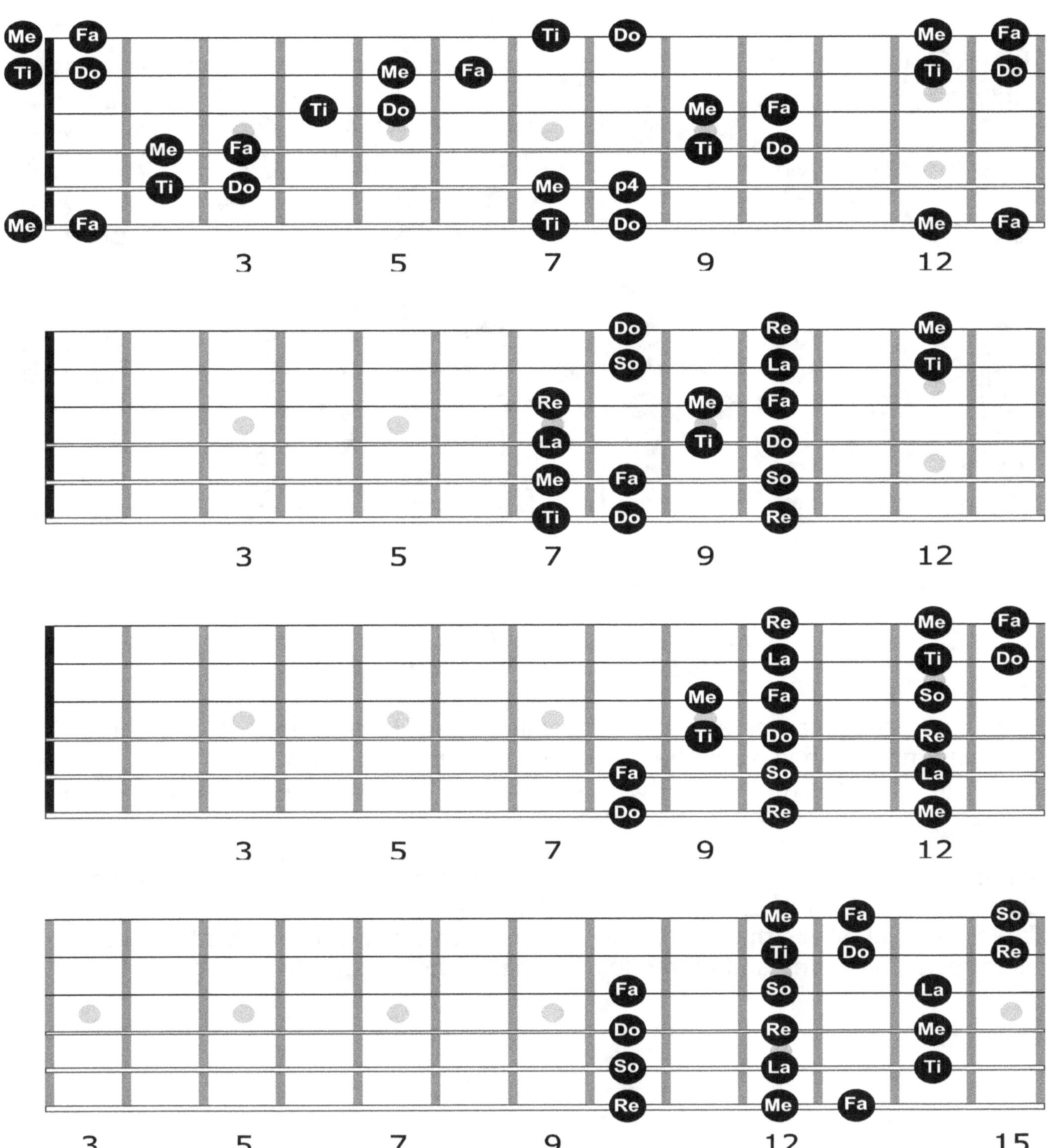

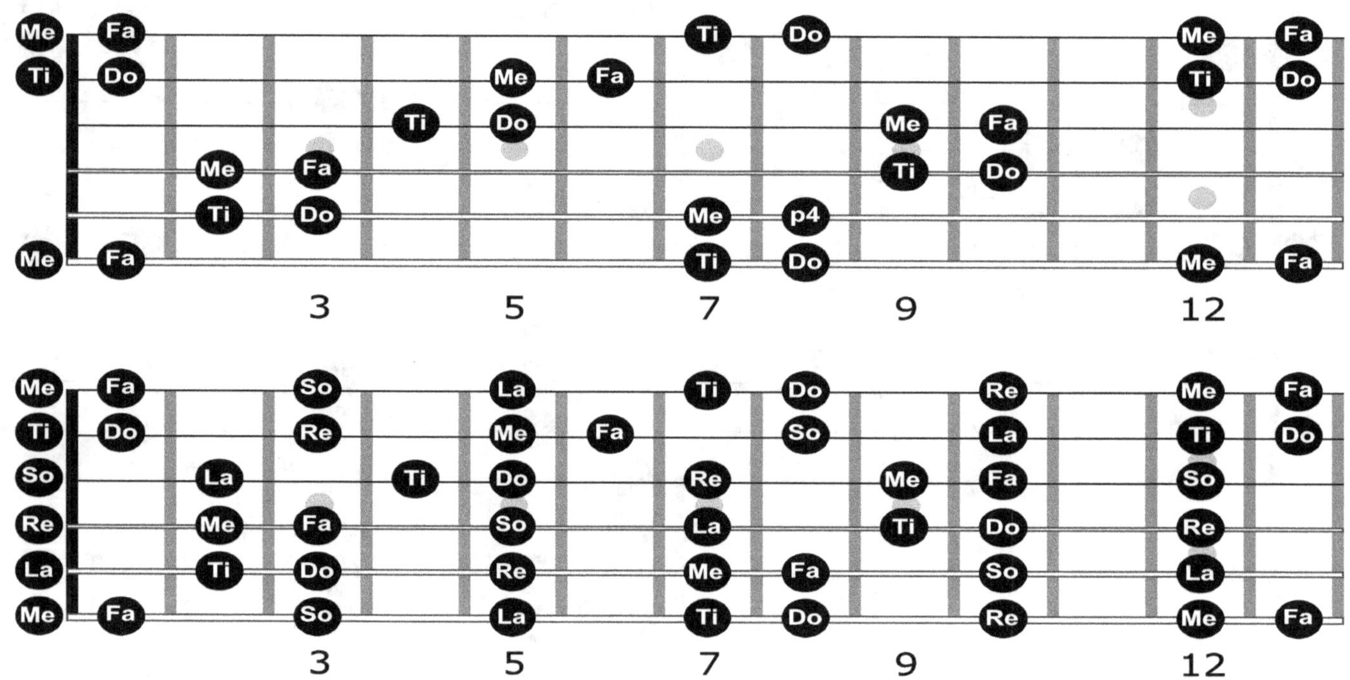

Modes and how to Play and Visualize Them

Each open string can be a mode if you think about how a mode is structured. The sixth and first strings would be the Phrygian mode. The fifth string is the Aeolian mode. The fourth string is the Dorian mode. The third string is the Mixolydian mode. The second string is the Locrian mode.

A mode can be played on single strings, a string pair, or string group. The half steps will be found in every mode just placed in different places in the mode. This is why the half steps that have been taught with two horizontal patterns, can be used to visualize any and all modes, no matter how they are played.

Modes Shapes and Fingerings

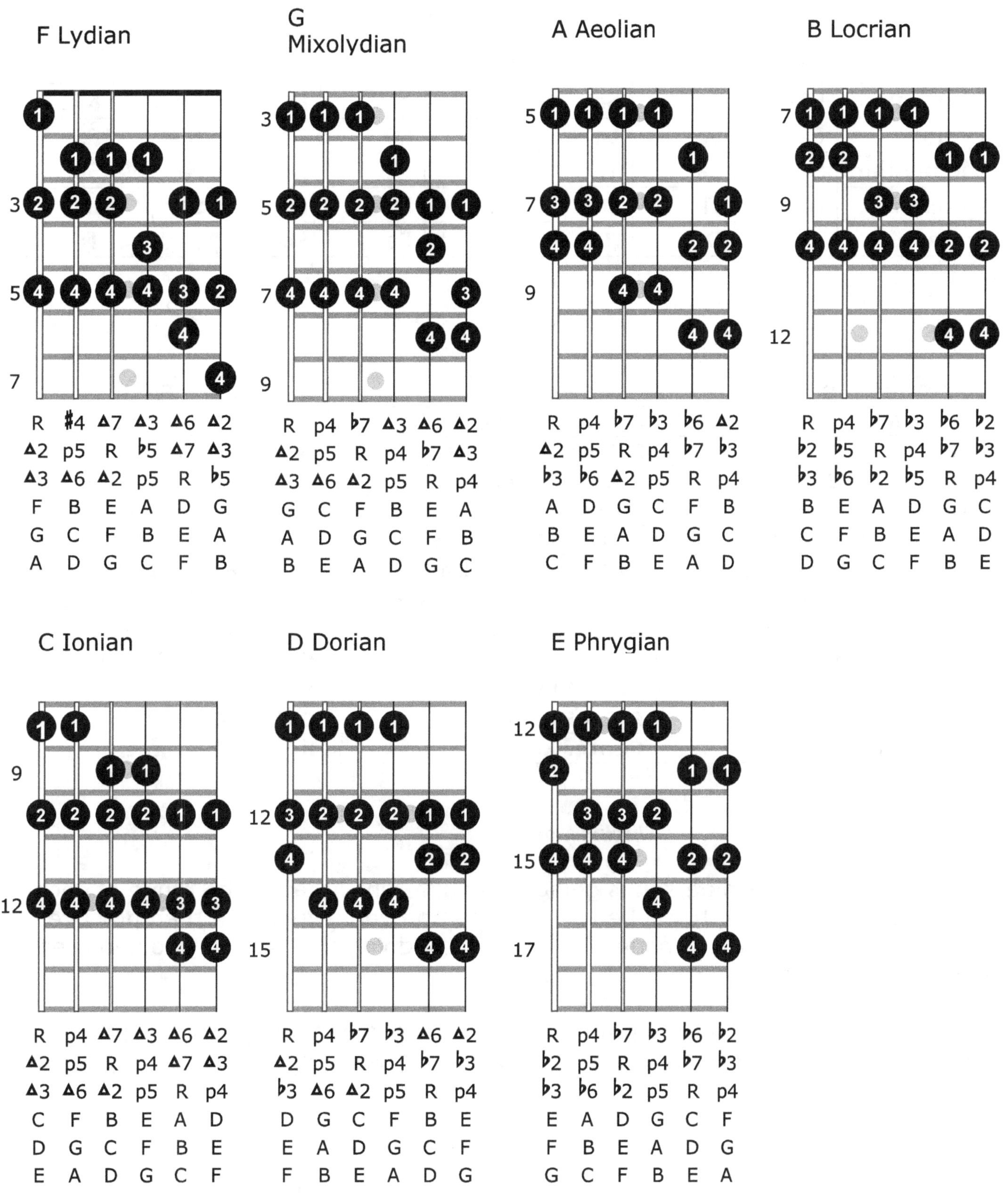

Ionian	Do	Re	Me	Fa	So	La	Ti	Do
Dorian	Re	Me	Fa	So	La	Ti	Do	Re
Phrygian	Me	Fa	So	La	Ti	Do	Re	Me
Lydian	Fa	So	La	Ti	Do	Re	Me	Fa
Mixolydian	So	La	Ti	Do	Re	Me	Fa	So
Aeolian	La	Ti	Do	Re	Me	Fa	So	La
Locrian	Ti	Do	Re	Me	Fa	So	La	Ti

F G A Bb C D E F	C D E F G A B C	G A B C D E F# G
C D E F G A B D	G A B C D E F# G	D E F# G A B C# D
G A B C D E F# G	D E F# G A B C# D	A B C# D E F# G# A
D E F# G A B C# D	A B C# D E F# G# A	E F# G# A B C# D# E
A B C# D E F# G# A	E F# G# A B C# D# E	B C# D# E F# G# A# B
E F# G# A B C# D# E	B C# D# E F# G# A# B	F# G# A# B C# D# E# F#
B C# D# E F# G# A# B	F# G# A# B C# D# E# F#	Db Eb F Gb Ab Bb C Db
Gb Ab Bb C Db Eb F G Ab	Db Eb F Gb Ab Bb C Db	Ab Bb C Db Eb F G Ab
Db Eb F Gb Ab Bb C Db	Ab Bb C Db Eb F G Ab	Eb F G Ab Bb C D Eb
Ab Bb C Db Eb F G Ab	Eb F G Ab Bb C D Eb	Bb C D Eb F G A Bb
Eb F G Ab Bb C D Eb	Bb C D Eb F G A Bb	F G A Bb C D E F
Bb C D Eb F G A Bb	F G A Bb C D E F	C D E F G A B C
Key to the left	**Center key**	**Key to the right**

Singing Modes for each person is going to be different because the range of each person is not the same. It will be up to you to find your range and then practice singing in that range each mode. The purpose of doing this is to develop your ear and help you be a better at writing melodies.

The Solfegio is a great way to practice singing modes and doing it around the circle is even better. The lessons with the close key modulations is excellent practice.

Ionian	Dorian	Phrygian	Lydian	Mixolydian	Aeolian	Locrian
C E G	D F A	E G B	F A C	G B D	A C E	B D F
G B D	A C E	B D F#	C E G	D F# A	E G B	F# A C
D F# A	E G B	F# A C#	G B D	A C# E	B D F#	C# E G
A C# E	B D F#	C# E G#	D F# A	E G# B	F# A C#	G# B D
E G# B	F# A C#	G# B D#	A C# E	B D# F#	C# E G#	D# F# A
B D# F#	C# E G#	D# F# A#	E G# B	F# A# C#	G# B D#	A# C# E
F# A# C#	G# B D#	A C# E#	B D# F#	C# E# G#	D# F# A#	E# G# B
Db F Ab	Eb Gb Bb	F Ab C	Gb Bb Db	Ab C Eb	Bb Db F	C Eb Gb
Eb G Bb	F Ab C	G Bb D	Ab C Eb	Bb D F	C Eb G	D F Ab
Bb D F	C Eb G	D F A	Eb G Bb	F A C	G Bb D	A C Eb
F A C	G Bb D	A C E	Bb D F	C E G	D F A	E G Bb

Ionian	Dorian	Phrygian	Lydian	Mixolydian	Aeolian	Locrian
Dorian	Phrygian	Lydian	Mixolydian	Aeolian	Locrian	Ionian
Phrygian	Lydian	Mixolydian	Aeolian	Locrian	Ionian	Dorian
Lydian	Mixolydian	Aeolian	Locrian	Ionian	Dorian	Phrygian
Mixolydian	Aeolian	Locrian	Ionian	Dorian	Phrygian	Lydian
Aeolian	Locrian	Ionian	Dorian	Phrygian	Lydian	Mixolydian
Locrian	Ionian	Dorian	Phrygian	Lydian	Mixolydian	Aeolian

Modal Chord Scales

Starting each mode with the root chord and completing the other six chords is how you would play the modal chord scale. The two tables above illustrate how you can play in every key, and the modal chord scales in that key.

These two tables will help you apply chords to your melodies if you want to compose melodies that use modes. In every major scale you have three major chords and three minor chords, and one diminished chord. The six other modes just shift those major and minor chords around to create the chord scales.

As you begin your study in modes it should be noted it is a far more extensive venture than what one can put in a few pages. May teachers on-line teach extensive lessons on modes. One I recommend looking at is Rick Beato. He is a great theory teacher and player. He has a lot of videos on modes.

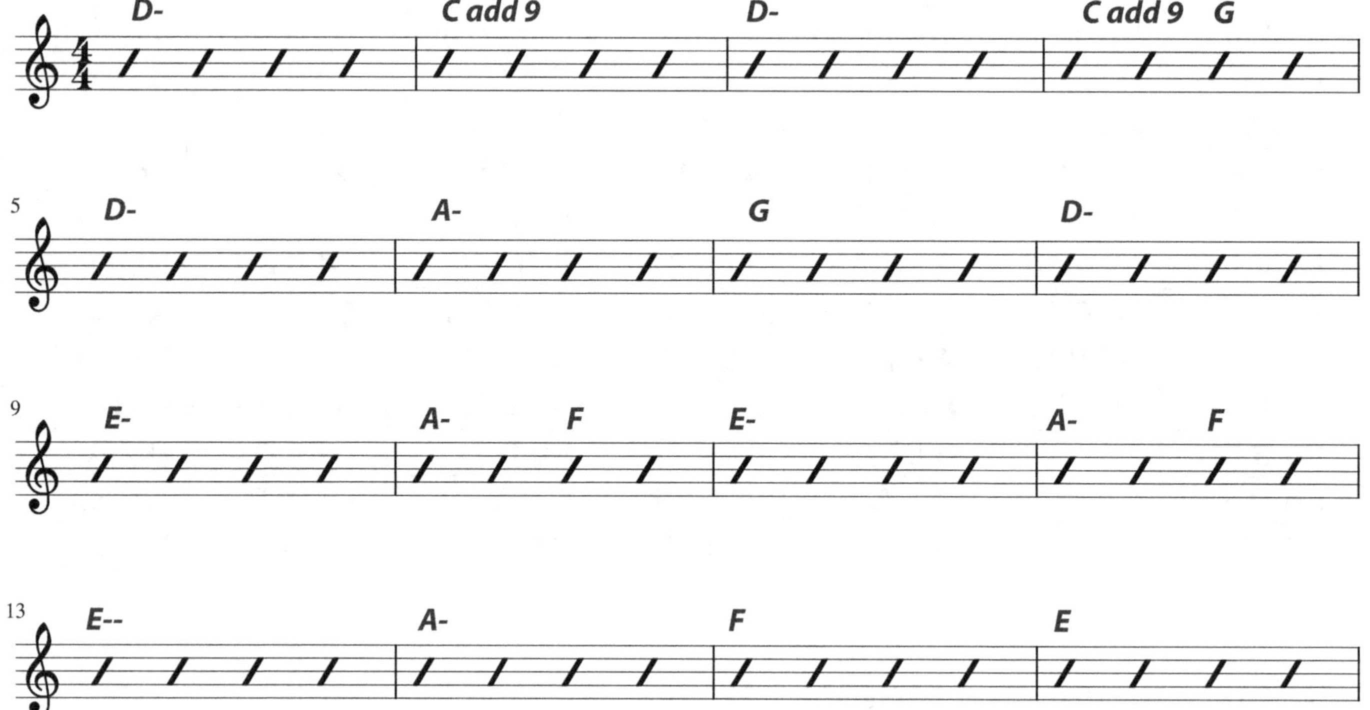

Composing in Dorian and Phrygian Modes

Begin, by singing the Dorian mode over the first eight bars, and then the Phrygian mode over the second eight bars.

The first example is based around the D minor chord. This would be an example of D Dorian minor. Try singing the melody phrases (Re Me Fa Re), (Re Me So Fa Re), and (Re La So Fa Re) as you play the loop. Notice, the emphasis for the melody is on Re (D).

The second loop is based around the E minor Phrygian. The E minor chord is where the loop starts and ends on. Sing these phrases over this loop, (Me La So Me) (Me La Fa Me), and (Me La Ti So Me).

Sing your own ideas over the chords and mix the progressions up and put them in different order but keep the emphasis on the root chord of each mode.

Composing in Lydian and Mixolydian

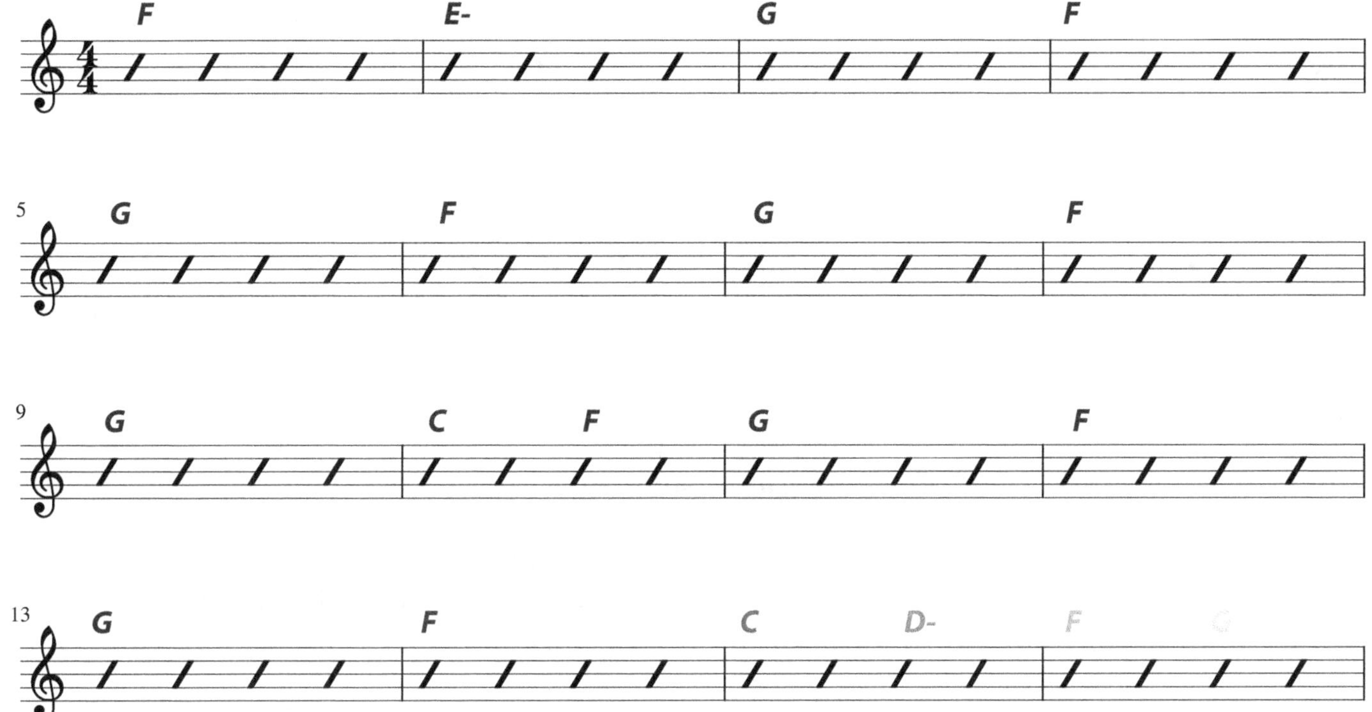

Composing in Lydian and Mixolydian Modes

Begin, by singing the Lydian mode over the first example, and then the Mixolydian mode over the second example.

The first eight bars is the Lydian mode, and its based around the F Lydian mode. Try singing (Fa So Me Fa), (Fa La Ti So Fa) (Fa Me Ti So Fa).

The second eight bars is the G Mixolydian mode. A lot of songs on the radio are Mixolydian. Try singing (So So Ti La So), (So Re Ti La So), (So Fa Ti La So).

Composing in Dorian and Phrygian

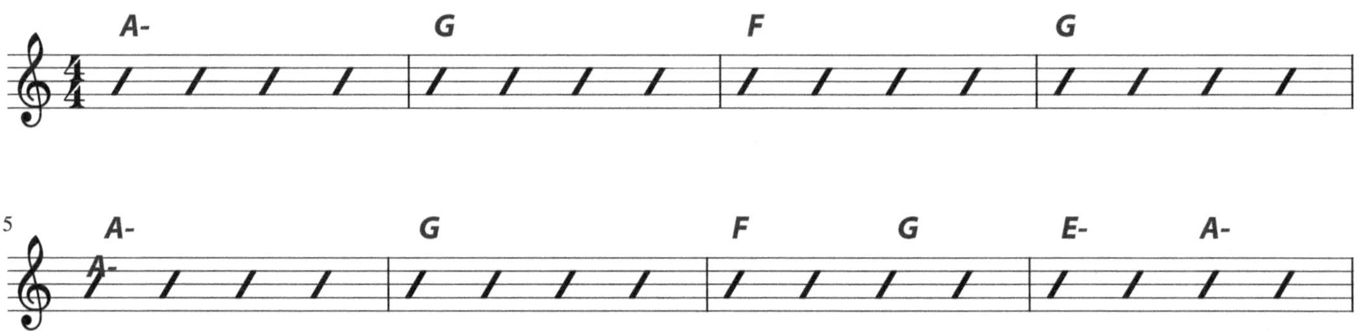

Composing in Aeolian

Begin, by singing the Aeolian mode over this example. By now you should see the pattern of what you are trying to do. Get the sound of each mode in your ears, and then create your own melodies from the examples you have been given.

This last example is based around the A minor chord. This would be an example of the A Aeolian minor mode. Try singing the melody phrases (La Ti So La), (La Re Ti Do La), and (La So La Ti So La) as you play the loop based around the A minor Aeolian mode.

The Aeolian mode is used in a lot of pop rock, and metal songs. Most all the modes are used in pop, with the exception of the Locrian mode. This mode is not used very often.

The locrian mode is based around the diminish triad. This is a triad with a minor third, and flat fifth (diminished (fifth). In strict music theory a fifth is called diminished. In jazz and street theory its called a flat fifth. No examples will be given with the locrian mode.

As with all the examples given, sing your own ideas over the chords and mix the progressions up, but keep the emphasis on the root chord of the Aeolian mode

Key and Chord Function	One, Three, Six	Four, Two, Six	Five, Two, Seven
Key of C	(C E G) (E G B) (A C E)	(F A C) (D F A) (A C E)	(G B D) (D F A) (G B D)

C- Ionian	D	E	F	G	A	B	C
D- Dorian	E	F	G	A	B	C	D
E- Phrygian	F	G	A	B	C	D	E
F- Lydian	G	A	B	C	D	E	F
G- Mixolydian	A	B	C	D	E	F	G
A-Aeolian	B	C	D	E	F	G	A
B-Locrian	C	D	E	F	G	A	B

Modes and Harmony

There are only seven different notes in each key, and a mode is the same seven notes starting and ending on any one of those notes in scale form. The mode creates a different feel then just the major scale or Ionian mode. You have learned some of the notes in the one chord are repeated in the three and six chords and can be used to substitute for the one. The notes other than the root of the key of (C), can also be thought of as being harmonized with the mode that would be the root of that
mode, as in E, now functioning as the E minor Phrygian mode.

The E note is in the C major, E minor, and A minor chords so, it could be harmonized with any one of those chords. If the melody is centered around the E, the E minor chord would function as the root of E minor Phrygian, and the melody would have a darker sound than C major. The same would be true if the E note were in the melody but the main point of harmonic interest was on the A note, then that would create an A Aeolian minor feel.

A mode is expressed by the emphasis being on that note that is the root of the mode as well as notes that are characteristic of that mode. Harmonizing that mode would use chords that normally start on the modes root and end on it. As I mentioned earlier a look at modal teaching as its own study is recommended and I suggest watching many of Rick Beato videos and his videos on modes.

There are seven notes in the major key, and six different notes you can use modally other than the major scale that is root of the key. The mode starting on the root of the major key is called the Ionian mode. These modes determine the feel of your composition. The brighter sounding modes are found on the roots of the major chords in the key. The Ionian mode, Lydian mode, and Mixolydian mode will be the brighter sounding melodies and harmonies with chords. The Dorian, Phrygian, Aeolian, and Locrian modes are the darker in sound modes. This knowledge helps you determine the direction you want to take in composing songs.

If you sit down to write a song that have lyrics that are sad, you will not put the happier modes to those lyrics and vice versa with the darker modes for happy lyrics. The modes create the overall feel of the song you are composing. Most of the examples up till this section on the modes, were based around the Ionian mode.

Song sections can be based on modes, or the entire song can stay in the sane mode. Modes can help you compose songs in so many ways one of the main advantages is to organize your thoughts. There is more to learn about modes than what has been covered here so far. All the information covered at this point has been based around modes from the major key, and its seven modes.

In summary of this brief look at modes you can take away these important points. Each mode has its own characteristic sound to it and is related to the parent major key. All the chords can be practiced in the major key in chord scale form. For example, starting on C you would play C major, D minor, E minor, F major, G major, A minor, and B diminish, as the Ionian chord scale. The Dorian chord scale would start on D minor and continue through all the chords from D minor, this would be the Dorian minor chord scale. The chord extensions would apply to the chords as well for the modes.

Any mode can be played in single strings, string pairs, or groups of strings. The patterns that have three notes per string are not really modal scales unless you start on the root and end on the root. The three note per string forms only scratch the service of how modal scales can and are played. These patterns are how many guitar players uses the fretboard to play modes today, and create modal melodies. It is very important to sing the modes to get the sound of them in your ears so you can determine what mode you want to use in your compositions.

Introduction to Modes

Modes were introduced and explained in diatonic keys. Then all twelve keys were shown.

Playing Modes

How modes are played on the guitar was illustrated with three notes on each string with seven modes for C and their fingerings were shown with diagrams.

Composing in the Various Modes

Modes Dorian, Phrygian, Lydian, Mixolydian, and Aeolian were used to give you ideas of how to compose songs in those modes. Composing melodies in modes was shown using solfegio.

Modal Harmony

How to use chords with modes was illustrated and the triads for every mode in all twelve keys was shown with a table to use as a reference.

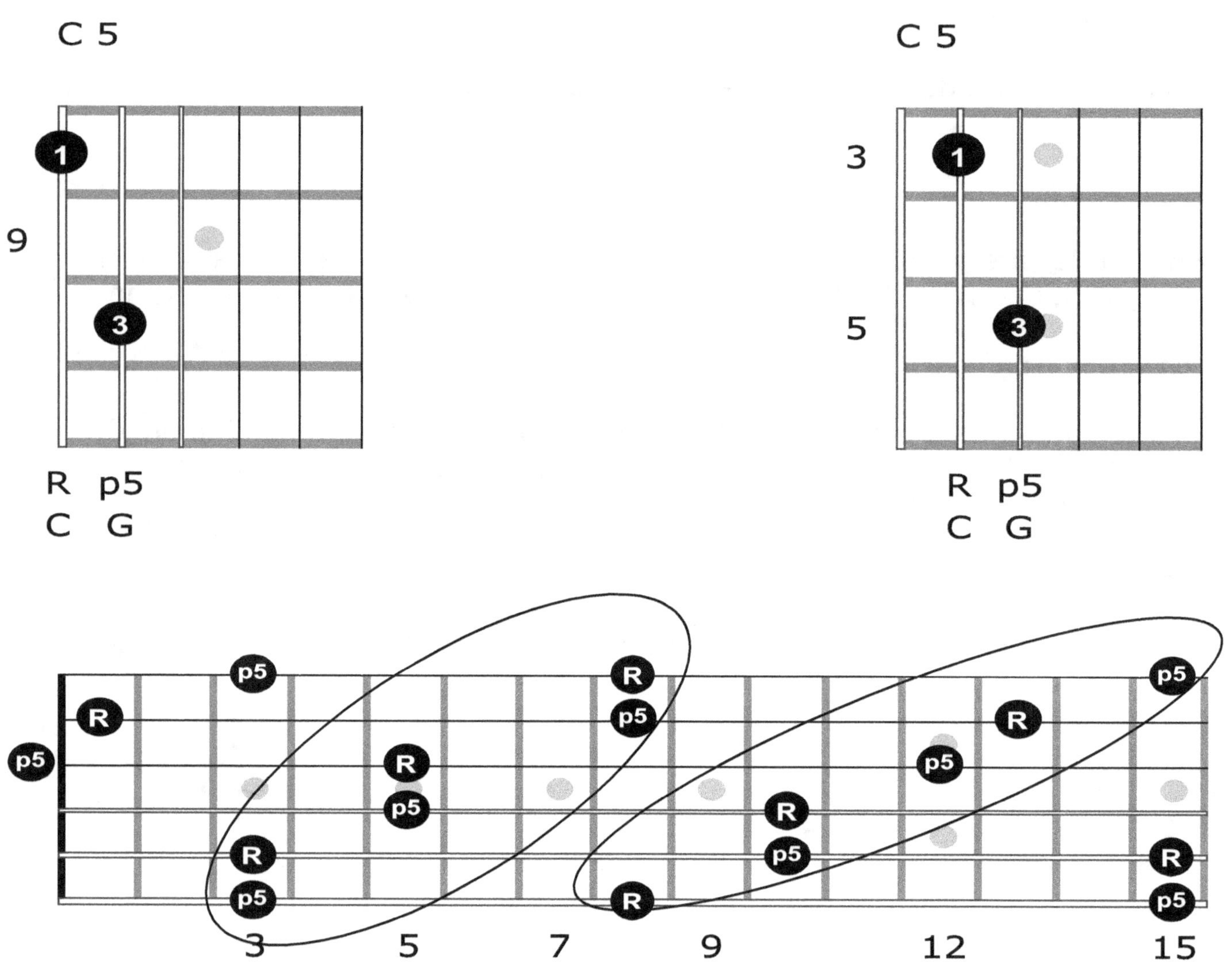

Power Chords

Power chords are defined as the root and fifth of a chord. The third is missing so they are neither major nor minor chords. But they can be played with the roots of all six chords in a major key. The intervals of root and fifth, form two visual patterns on the fretboard. Where the root of the power chord is and where the fifth of the power chord is, mark the locations on the sixth string to visualize the two different patterns that halve ovals around them.

Bb 5

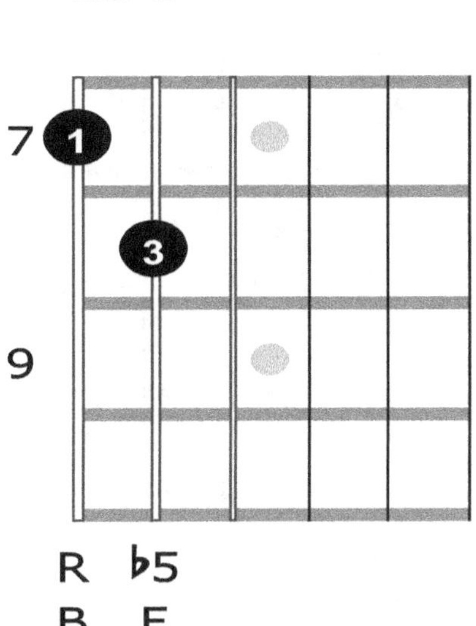

Bb5 5

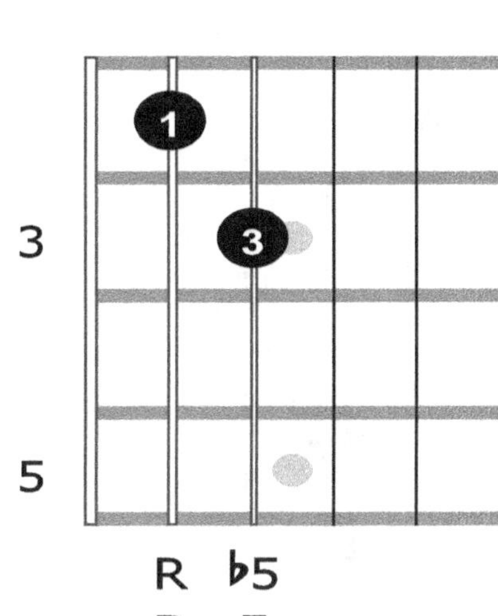

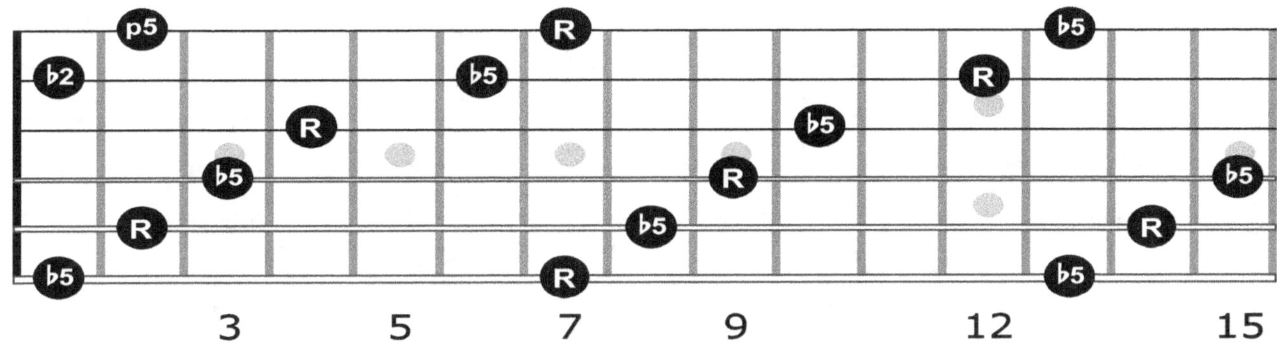

Flat Five Power Chords

The flat five power chord has the fifth lowered a half step. The two visual patterns it forms are on the seventh of the major key, in the key of C that would be the note B, and the flat fifth note F. Normally from B it would be F# in the major key of B. Since there are no Sharps in the key of C, F will be a natural note. Notice, the two patterns are identical.

Bb 5

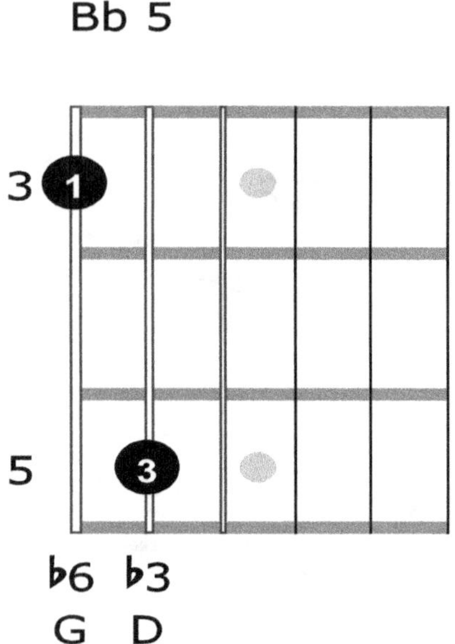

Bb5 5

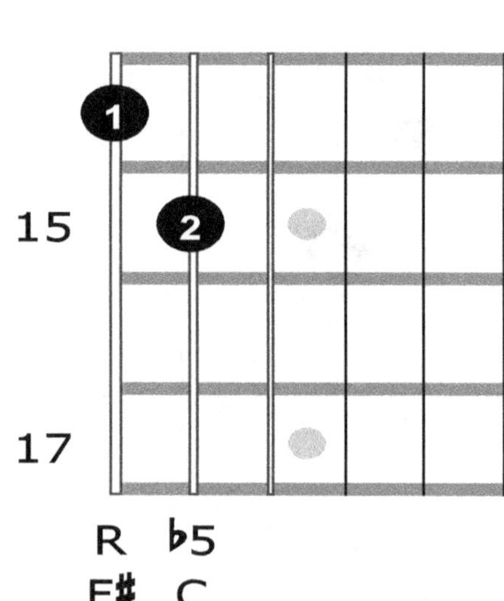

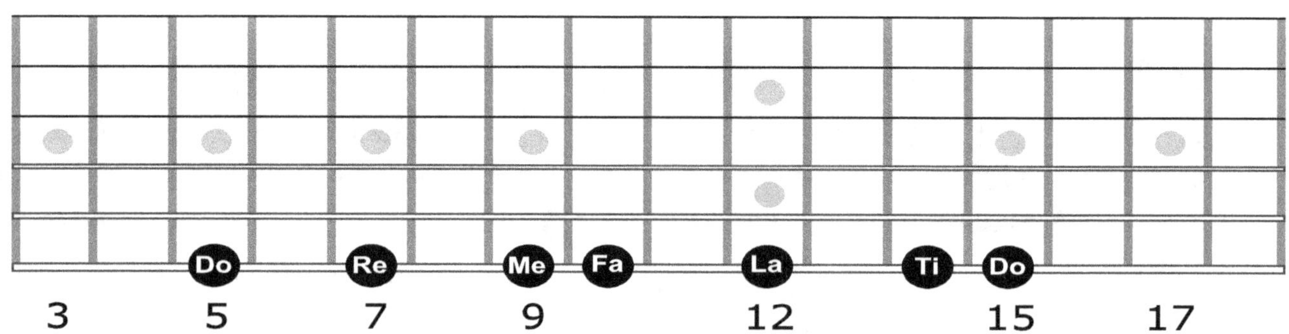

Using Power Chords and Why

Power chords can be played in chord scale form. The G, A, B, C, D, and E power chords would be played using the first power chord fingering on the fret locations on the diagram with Do, through La. The Ti power chord would use the second diagram fingering.

These power chords can be moved to the fifth string. To play the C major power chord scale. Move them again to the fourth string root to play the F major power chord scale. The lesson on the circle of fifths can help you play power chords in every key. All string transferring of thees power chords would uses the same finger patterns.

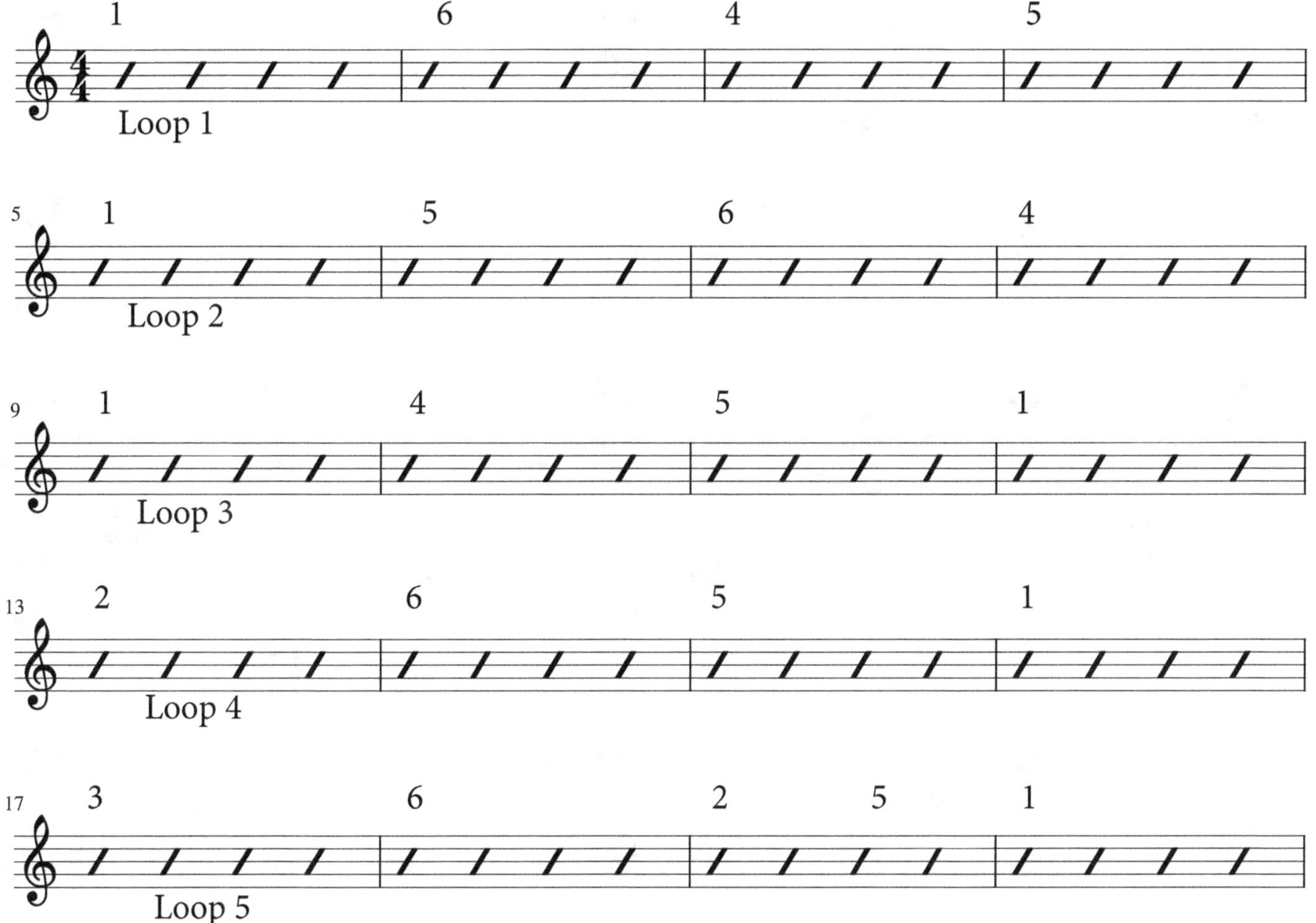

Using Power Chords and Why

Writing something that sounds edgy or in a rock, metal feel you want to many times avoid chords with thirds. This is where you use the power chord. The absence of the third in the chord sounds heavier or harder in the feel of what you apply power chords too. All the loops and things you have leaned can be played with power chords. Remember the power chord is just the root and fifth of the chord.

Songs often use a mixture of power chords and basic triads in the them. The first section of a song may have basic chords, then switch to power chords to get a heavier and harder feel.

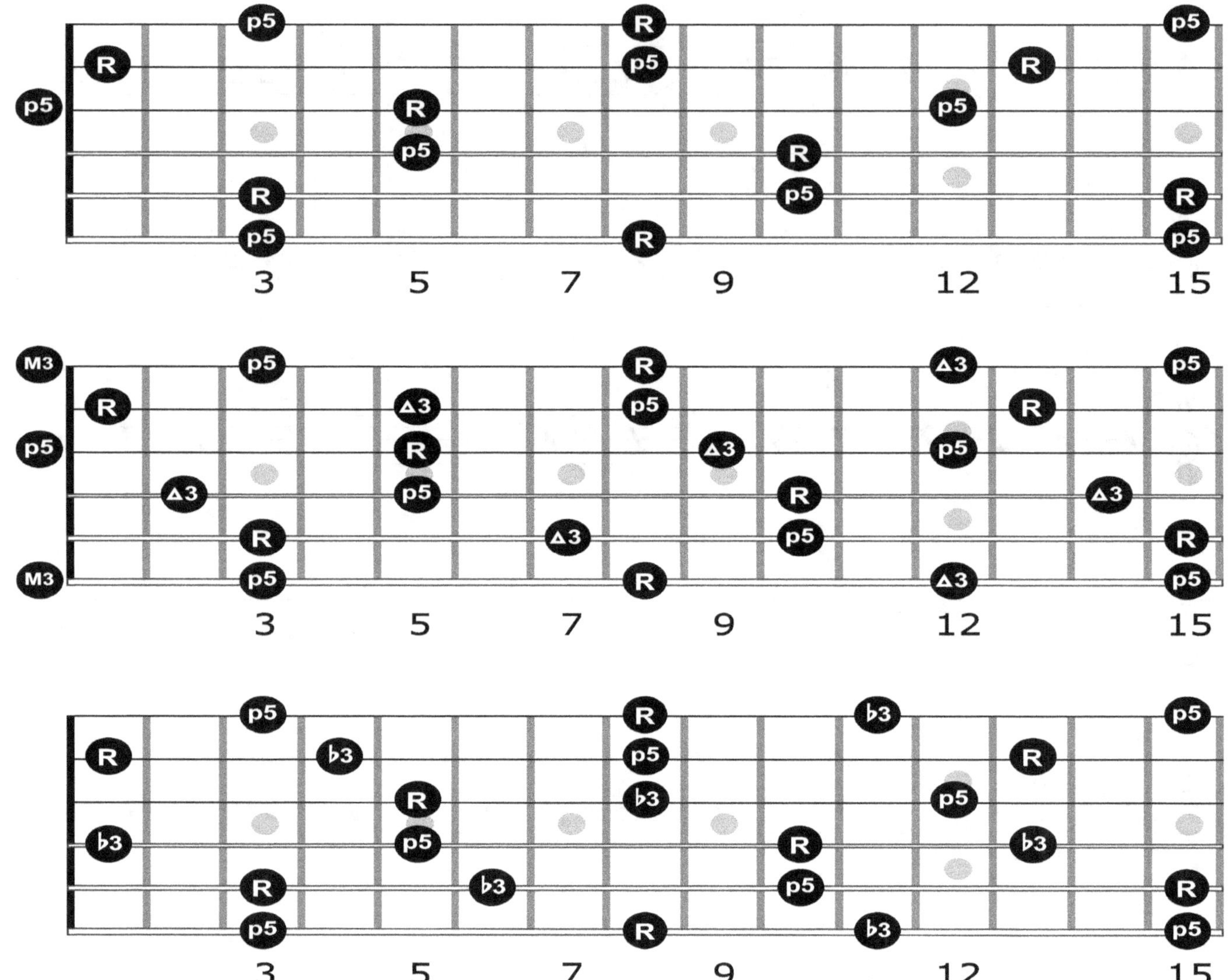

Visualizing Chords

Slash chords can be thought of as inversions too. A chord can have the third, fifth and even the extension as the lowest note. Being able to visualize all the notes in full fretboard form, will help you with slash chords, with the basic triads. Then you can apply the extension as the lowest note much easier for those slash chords.

To learn to visualize the slash chords start with the root and fifth that you have learned for the power chord. The two full fretboard triads are major and minor.

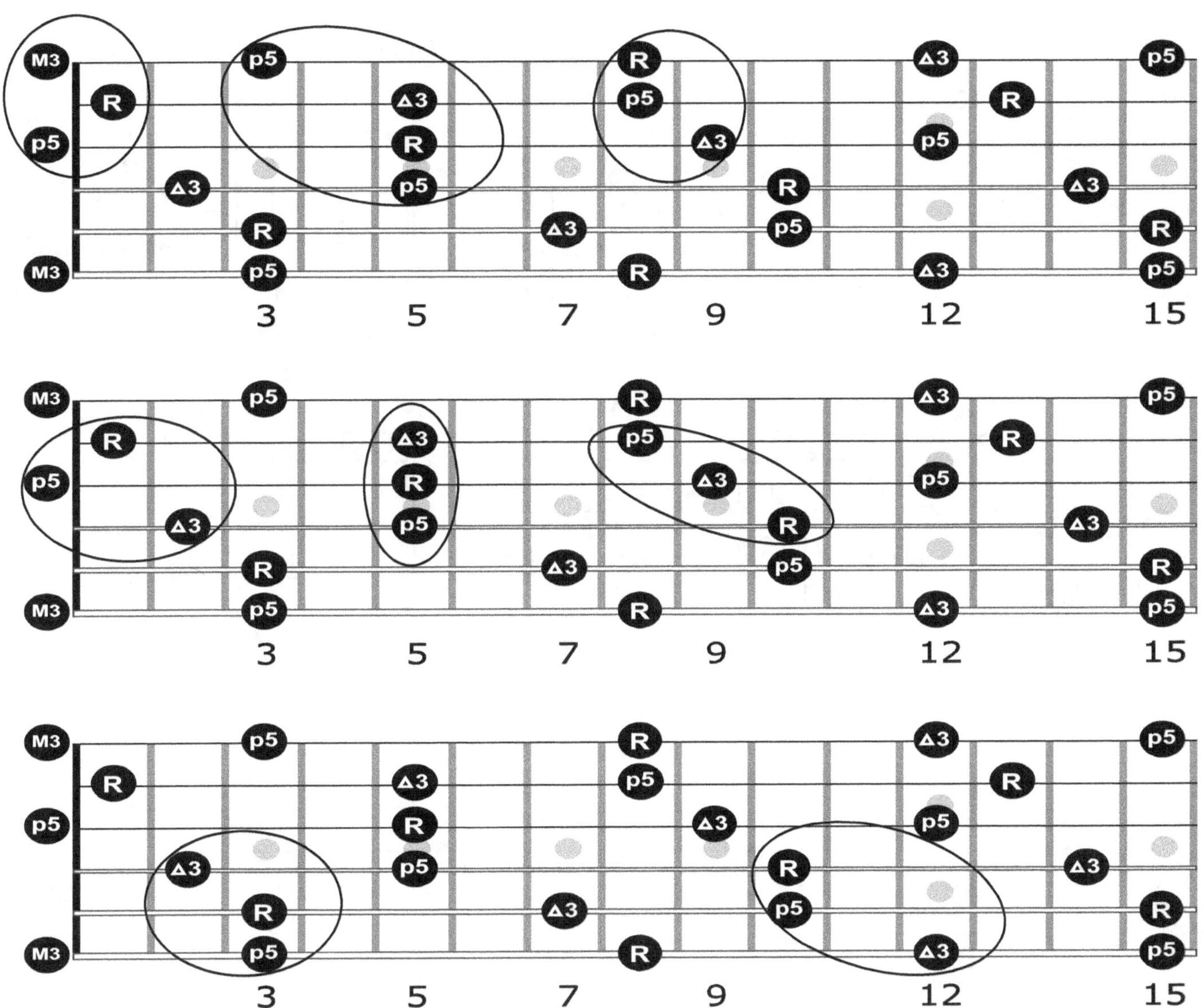

Slash Chords

The three diagrams illustrate slash chords with three strings in three different string groups. The first diagram stays on the first three strings. The first chord is written as C/G, this means the G is the lowest note. The next chord is in root position. The third chord is C/E, meaning the E is the lowest note.

The second diagram stays on the middle three strings, and illustrates slash chords C/E, C/G, and root position. The third diagram illustrates, C/G, C in root position, and C/E.

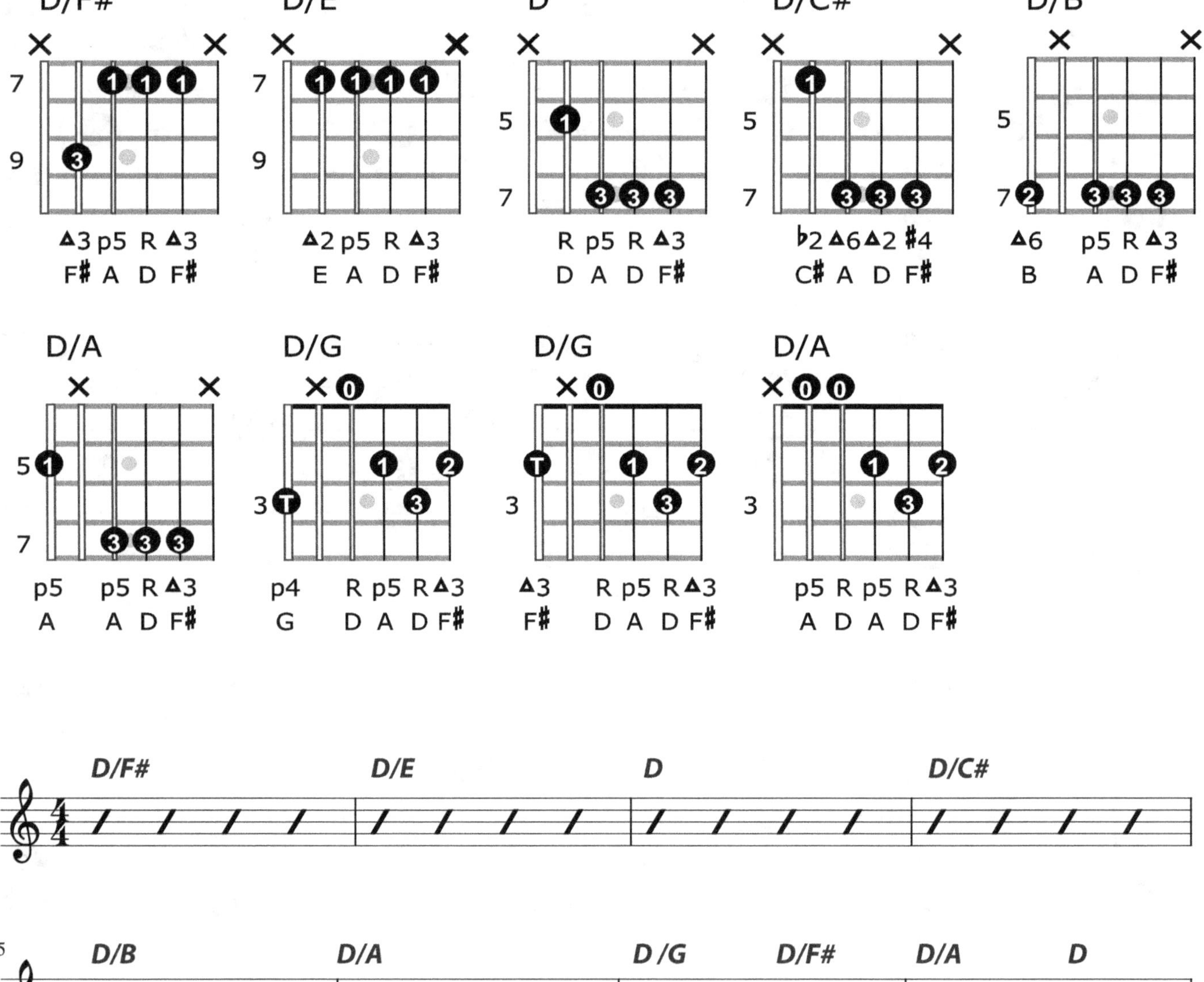

Slash Chords Over D

The example here, is illustrating how the D chord is played with a descending bass line over the chord. This is one way slash chords are used. This is also called pedal point, because the chord remains the same as the bass notes over the chord change.

The slash chords in this example should give you a good idea of how to use them if you want a descending bass line over a chord. The chord shapes must be moved in order to uses a descending bass line . Use the chord diagrams to read each measure. The last D chord should be in the open position that you already have learned.

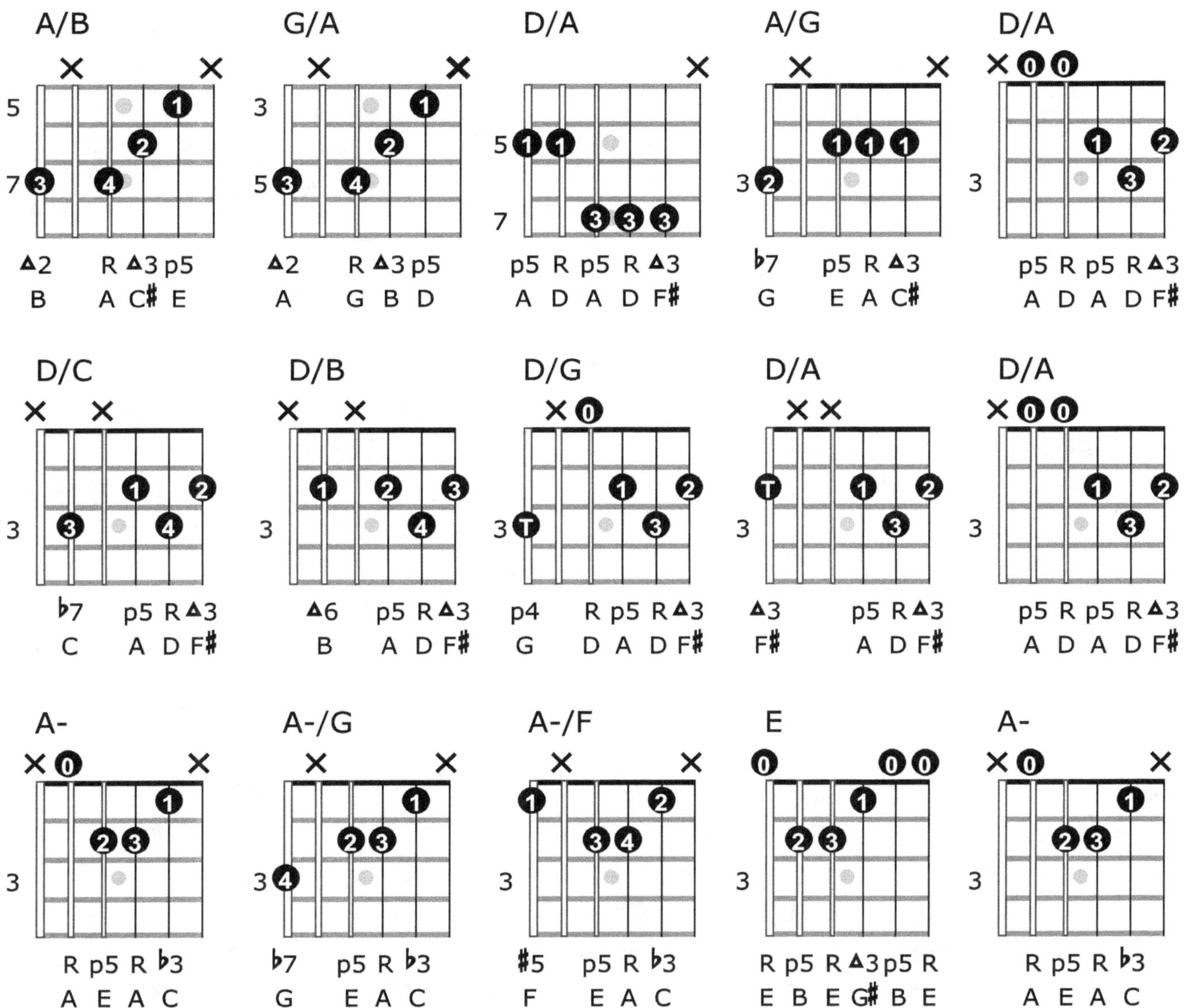

Slash Chord Cliches

These examples are to be played as three separate applications. The first one is in D, the second one is in G, and the last one is in A minor. All three examples are fragments of how many song writers have used slash chords, in their song writing. All three are very pop and rock cliches.

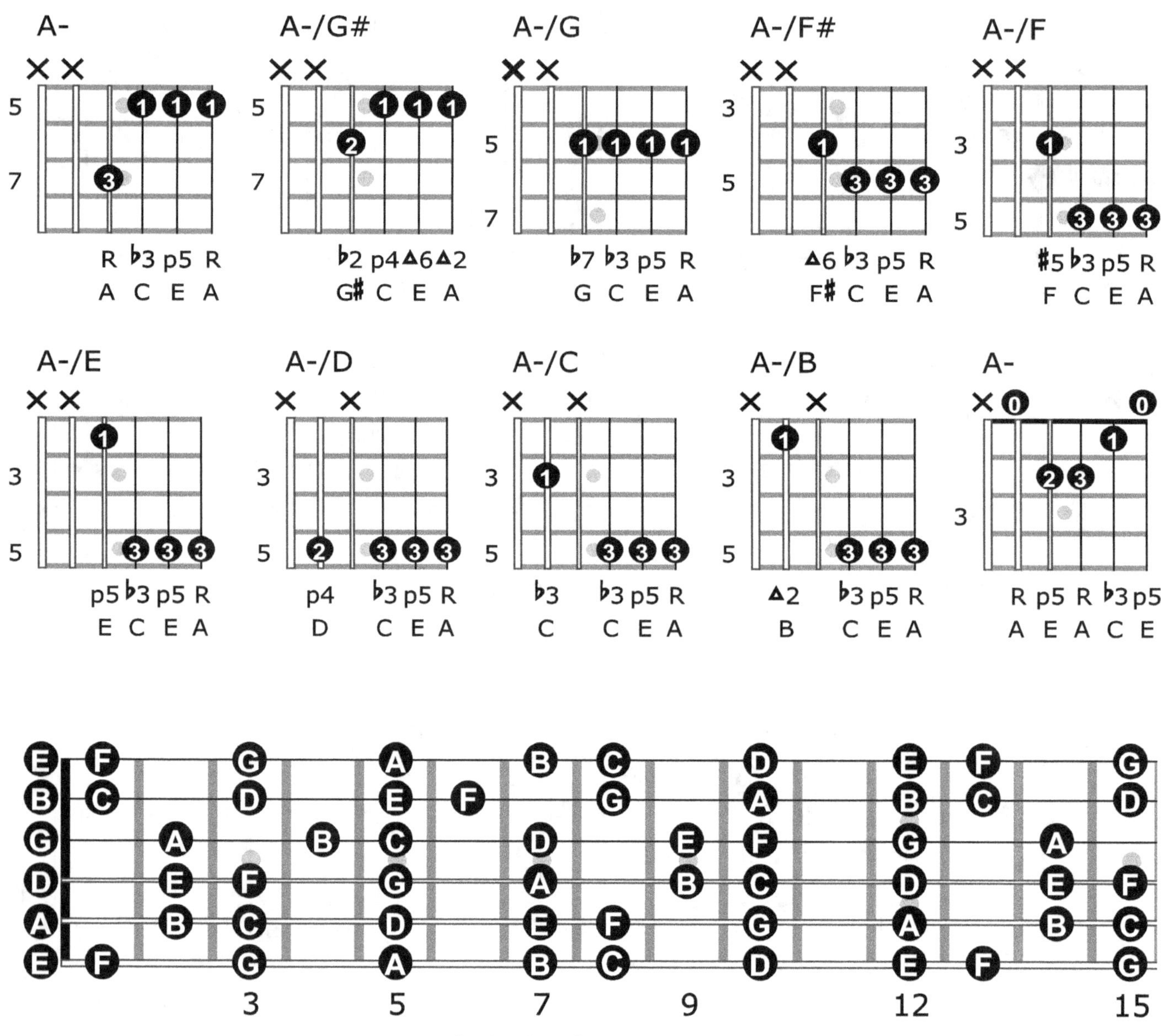

Slash Chords Over D

Th Your ability to play slash chords is going to depend a lot on how well you know the fretboard. With the two notes G#, and F#, all the other chords have the notes from the key of C in this example. Having the ability to see the way bass notes are used over chords from the full fretboard image gives you access to any type of slash chord you want to play.

 Look at the full fretboard and follow the slash chords above it and see if you can see them inside of the full fretboard image.
The slash chord example here is another widely used sequence. This example took it all the way to A an octave lower. But you can hear this example in fragments instead of going to the octave.

It should be mentioned that you can use a capo with all these slash chords.

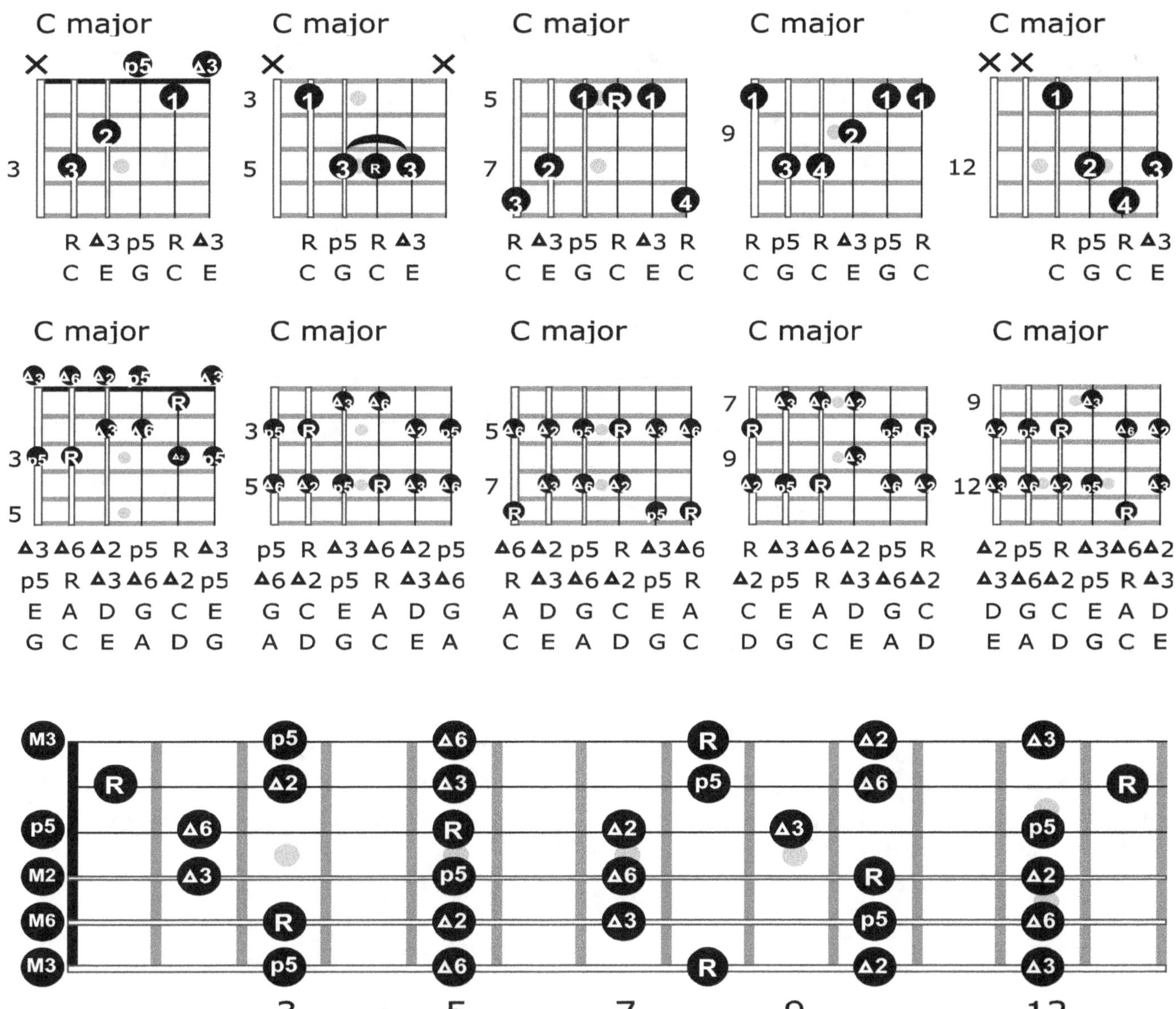

Pentatonic Scales

The major scale has seven notes, when you remove the fourth and seventh notes what remains is the root, second, third, fifth, and sixth notes of the scale, creating the five-note scale, called the major pentatonic scale. What is on this page is what most guitarist know is the five major pentatonic shapes that are close to the major chord.

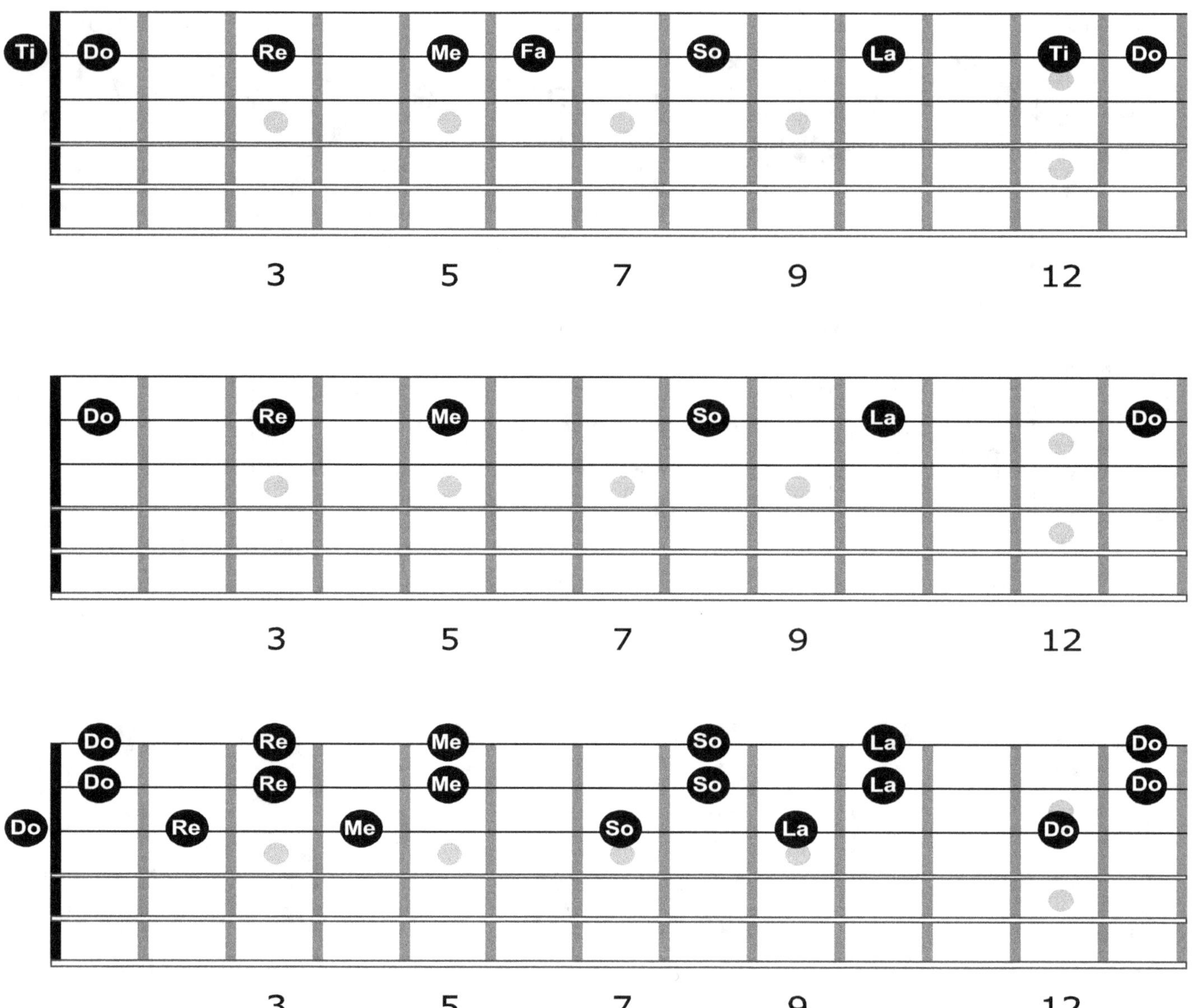

Pentatonic Scales and Keys

The major scale has seven notes, when you remove the fourth and seventh notes what remains is the root, second, third, fifth, and sixth notes of the scale, creating the five-note scale, called the major pentatonic scale.

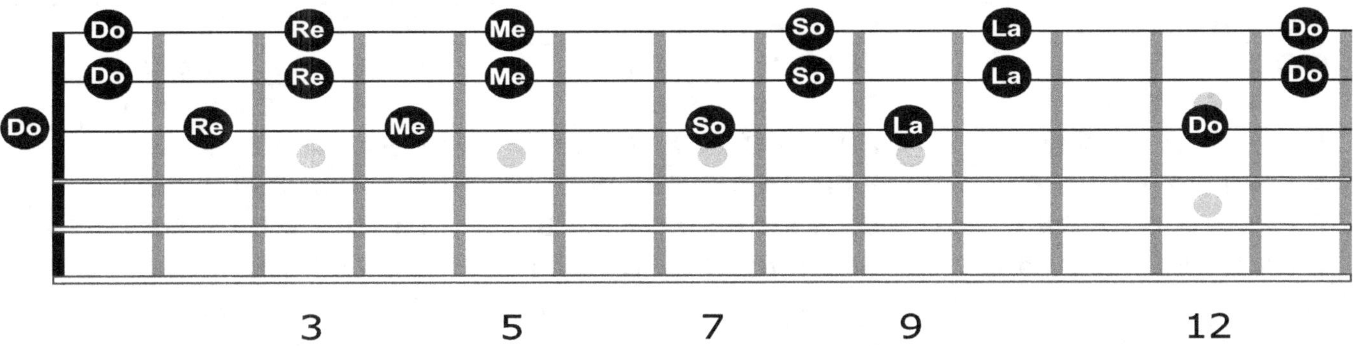

Ionian	M 2	M 2	m 2	M 2	M 2	M 2	m 2
Dorian	M 2	m 2	M 2	M 2	M 2	m 2	M 2
Phrygian	m 2	M 2	M 2	M 2	m 2	M 2	M 2
Lydian	M 2	M 2	M 2	m 2	M 2	M 2	m 2
Mixolydian	M 2	M 2	m 2	M 2	M 2	m 2	M 2
Aeolian	M 2	m 2	M 2	M 2	m 2	M 2	M 2
Locrian	m 2	M 2	M 2	m 2	M 2	M 2	M 2

C- Ionian	D	E	F	G	A	B	C
D- Dorian	E	F	G	A	B	C	D
E- Phrygian	F	G	A	B	C	D	E
F- Lydian	G	A	B	C	D	E	F
G- Mixolydian	A	B	C	D	E	F	G
A-Aeolian	B	C	D	E	F	G	A
B-Locrian	C	D	E	F	G	A	B

Pentatonic Scales and Modes

C major pentatonic has the very same notes as A minor pentatonic. The F major pentatonic is the same as D minor pentatonic. G major pentatonic is the same as E minor pentatonic. The notes of C major pentatonic and A minor pentatonic are found in the C Ionian mode, and the A minor Aeolian mode. The notes of F major pentatonic are in the F Lydian mode, and the D Dorian mode. The notes in the G major pentatonic are in the G Mixolydian mode and the E Phrygian

F G A Bb C D E F	C D E F G A B C	G A B C D E F# G
C D E F G A B D	G A B C D E F# G	D E F# G A B C# D
G A B C D E F# G	D E F# G A B C# D	A B C# D E F# G# A
D E F# G A B C# D	A B C# D E F# G# A	E F# G# A B C# D# E
A B C# D E F# G# A	E F# G# A B C# D# E	B C# D# E F# G# A# B
E F# G# A B C# D# E	B C# D# E F# G# A# B	F# G# A# B C# D# E# F#
B C# D# E F# G# A# B	F# G# A# B C# D# E# F#	Db Eb F Gb Ab Bb C Db
Gb Ab Bb C Db Eb F G Ab	Db Eb F Gb Ab Bb C Db	Ab Bb C Db Eb F G Ab
Db Eb F Gb Ab Bb C Db	Ab Bb C Db Eb F G Ab	Eb F G Ab Bb C D Eb
Ab Bb C Db Eb F G Ab	Eb F G Ab Bb C D Eb	Bb C D Eb F G A Bb
Eb F G Ab Bb C D Eb	Bb C D Eb F G A Bb	F G A Bb C D E F
Bb C D Eb F G A Bb	F G A Bb C D E F	C D E F G A B C
Key to the left	**Center key**	**Key to the right**

Pentatonic Scales and Circle of Fifths

The notes in C major pentatonic can also belong to F Mixolydian, and A minor Phrygian modes. The notes in C major pentatonic are also in the C Lydian mode and the A minor Dorian modes. The understanding here is the five notes C D E G A, are in all the modes mentioned. Which means the C major pentatonic scale could be in the keys of F and G major both. So, if you compose a melody that uses C major pentatonic, you could harmonize it with chords from the keys of C, F, and G.

The modes in the key of C, also contain F major pentatonic, and G major pentatonic, but in the key of F you would not have the G major pentatonic and the E minor pentatonic. In the key of G you would not have F major pentatonic or D minor pentatonic.

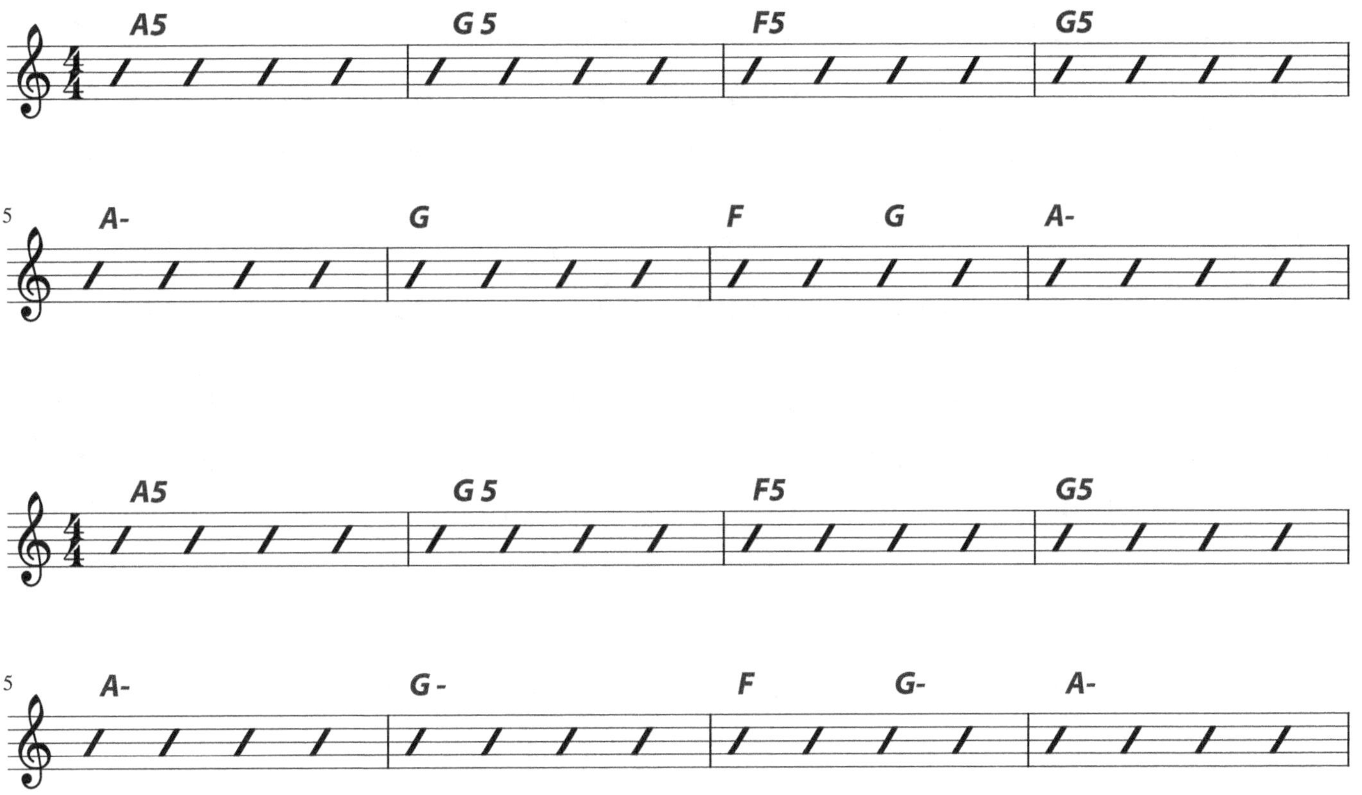

Pentatonic Scales and Modes

The power chords A, G, and F can be in the keys of C and F, therefor the melody that is under them can be in both those keys. The modes in C and pentatonic scales in C can all be used and the same with the modes. When the thirds are added they define the key in the first example as C.

The second example, is illustrating that the chord G minor is defining the key of F. This is because G minor has Bb in it as the third of that chord. When the third is not present and only power chords are being used the actual key is often not so definite. This is what makes power chords so widely used in rock, and metal.

The pentatonic scales can be used as a melody over power chords because they can be in both keys C and F too. In both examples if only power chords were used, the notes in A minor (C major pentatonic) scales, and G major (E minor pentatonic) scales can be used. The second example over the G minor chord, the G minor (Bb major) pentatonic scales would be used.

C Ionian	C E G	D F A	E G B	F A C	G B D	A C E	B D F
C Dorian	C Eb G	D F A	Eb G Bb	F A C	G Bb D	A C Eb	Bb D F
C Phrygian	C Eb G	Db F Ab	Eb G Bb	F Ab C	G Bb Db	Ab C Eb	G Db Bb
C Lydian	C E G	D F# A	G B D	A C G	B D F#	C# E G	D F# A
C Mixolydian	C E G	D F A	E G Bb	F A C	G Bb D	A C E	Bb D F
C Aeolian	C Eb G	D F Ab	Eb G Bb	F Ab C	G Bb D	Ab C Eb	Bb D F
C Locrian	C Eb Gb	Db F Ab	Eb Gb Bb	F Ab C	Gb Bb Db	Ab C Eb	Bb Db F

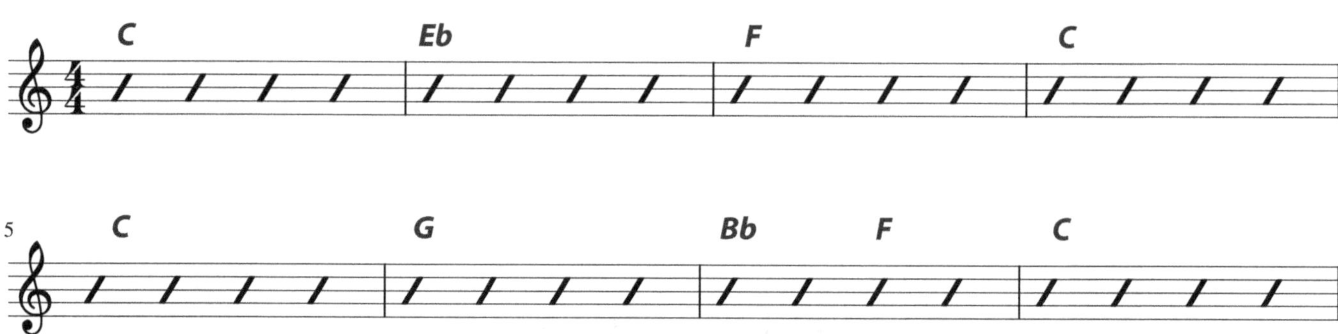

Composing with Modal Interchange.

Modal interchange or modal mixture are very advanced concepts of using modes. You can think of it as parallel modes. For example, if the note C was the root of every mode, you would have seven modes that start with C. The first mode would be C Ionian. The second mode would be C Dorian, and it's parent scale would be B flat major. The third mode would be C Phrygian, and it's parent scale would be A flat major. The 4th mode would be C Lydian, the C Lydian's parent scale would be G major. The C mixolydian scale, would be found in the F major scale. The C Aeolian mode Is the 6th mode and it's parent scale is the key E flat major. The 7th mode that starts with C is the C Locrian mode and it belongs to the key of C sharp, or D flat.

The example above borrows Eb from C minor Aeolian in the second measure. The Bb, is borrowed from C Mixolydian.

Modal interchange is another writing tool that could have a lot more information offered than this brief explanation Rick Beato has videos on this subject worth seeing.

Power Chords

The power chord was introduced in section seven, with how to visualize it first. The make up of the power chord is the root and fifth of any chord. The power chord does not have a third, so it is used in application in songs to make them sound heavy and edgy. The power chord can be used with melodies from two different keys because it does not have a third in it.

Slash Chords

Slash chords were discussed is section seven, and examples of application of slash chords were provided too. First tools to visualize all major and minor triads was given so the ability to see the possibilities of slash chords can be easier. The examples of slash chords, illustrate how they can be used to enhance your song writing, for introductions, outros, or all parts of your song. These examples are found in many popular songs.

Pentatonic Scales

Pentatonic scales are five note scales that are missing the third and seventh notes from the major scale or the second and sixth notes from the minor scale. The pentatonic scales also are found in the seven modes of each major key as well. The three major pentatonic scales are in the Ionian, Lydian, and Mixolydian modes. The three minor pentatonic scales are in the Dorian, Phrygian, and Aeolian modes. The notes of the major pentatonic scale in the Ionian mode, are the same notes in the Aeolian minor mode. The same holds true for the notes in Lydian mode, and Dorian mode, when pentatonic scales are concerned. The same rule applies for the Mixolydian mode, and Phrygian modes too when applying pentatonic scales.

Modal Interchange

Modal interchange was introduced with some Ideas for using it. The term borrowed chords is also used to describe modal interchange.

Nothing can replace inspiration when it comes to writing music, or art. Knowledge can help to inspire you at times, but many great songs were written by artist who know extraordinarily little about music or the guitar. So, it should always be understood that most of the greatest songs were from the composer being inspired.

The study of music can develop the ability to create inspiration, due to the mind and ears practicing things that great songs were written with. Through time patterns of chords, and scales that work are learned and then inspiration happens, and song ideas are birthed.

The song composing process can be studied as far as form goes, and certain rules established, but those rules can be broken too as artist create songs that require the boundaries to be pushed. Thus, composing a song should never be dictated by rules and forms that cannot be broken. Rules and forms provide guidelines to start with. But if a song has great melody and feel that extend beyond the normal set rules for measures and sections, an artist should follow their inspiration.

The pursuit of knowledge of the guitar and music is endless, and one does not need to know everything on the guitar to write great songs with chords and melodies. However, this book did provide a lot of information for learning the guitar, with the focus on writing songs. There is so much more to cover with song writing and playing the guitar than this volume 1 has laid out. This volume has covered a lot of information that should help you start to write great songs. You should be able to put chords and structure to your song.

Many of the chord progressions and ideas in this volume are found in famous songs, too numerous to mention. This book did not limit a writer to any one style but touched on things found in every style of songs being played today. One suggestion I can give is to listen to the kinds of music you want to write and imitate what you have heard with variations you have added. A lot of songs have been written through imitation. The information covered in this book, should help you to understand a lot of what you are hearing in songs you are trying to imitate. But, once again imitation cannot replace inspiration either.

I wish you the best, and if what you have learned here has helped you write your songs, then I know I put together a good book. Thanks for taking the time to go through this volume.

Sincerely Greg Brown